WHER
SOVEREIGNTY

power seeks to be exercised,
authority seeks assent.

authority is the moment that
disregarding a declaration becomes
not just ill-advised, but _wrong_.

authority = power + legitimacy.

The continued exercised power until
People give in.

The authority of power can only be
kept if power is continually _exercised_.

Columbia Studies in

Political Thought / Political History

Columbia Studies in Political Thought / Political History
Dick Howard, General Editor

Columbia Studies in Political Thought/Political History is a series dedicated to exploring the possibilities for democratic initiative and the revitalization of politics in the wake of the exhaustion of twentieth-century ideological "isms." By taking a historical approach to the politics of ideas about power, governance, and the just society, this series seeks to foster and illuminate new political spaces for human action and choice.

For the list of titles in this series see page 169.

The translation of this work was funded by Geisteswissenschaften International—Translation Funding for Work in the Humanities and Social Sciences from Germany, a joint initiative of the Fritz Thyssen Foundation, the German Federal Foreign Office, the collecting society VG WORT, and the Börsenverein des Deutschen Buchhandels (German Publishers & Booksellers Association).

SOVEREIGNTY

The Origin and Future
of a Political and Legal Concept

Dieter Grimm

Translated by Belinda Cooper

COLUMBIA UNIVERSITY PRESS
New York

Columbia University Press

Publishers Since 1893

New York   Chichester, West Sussex

cup.columbia.edu

Copyright © 2009 Berlin University Press

Copyright © 2015 Columbia University Press

Library of Congress Cataloging-in-Publication Data

Grimm, Dieter, 1937–

[Souveränität. English]

Sovereignty: the origin and future of a political and legal concept / Dieter Grimm;

Translated by Belinda Cooper.

pages cm. — (Columbia studies in political thought/political history)

Translated from German.

Includes bibliographical references and index.

ISBN 978-0-231-16424-5 (cloth: alk. paper) — ISBN 978-0-231-16425-2 (pbk.: alk.

paper) — ISBN 978-0-231-53930-2 (e-book)

1. Sovereignty. 2. State, The.   I. Title.

JC327.G7513 2015

320.1'5—dc23   2014041679

Printed in the United States of America

Cover & interior design: Martin N. Hinze

Contents

Series Editor's Foreword

The concept of sovereignty is associated with the emergence of the modern state. Today the sovereignty of that state appears to be threatened. On the one hand, the forces of the global market limit its ability to determine its own destiny and care for the welfare of its citizens. On the other hand, the growing weight of a cosmopolitan moral conscience weighs on the political choices of liberal democratic political institutions. The creation of international organizations to overcome these limitations founders on the ambiguity of their political status. Are these institutions simply the product of treaties made by states that retain their sovereignty, or do the have a universal validity that trumps the particular limits of their foundations? These contemporary challenges need to be examined from the perspective of the series Columbia Studies in Political Thought/Political History.

Dieter Grimm, a former judge on the German Constitutional Court and a professor of law, wrote this tightly argued study to counter the confusions that result from an ahistorical understanding of the concept of sovereignty. Although its modern formulation by Jean Bodin served to justify the absolute monarchy in France, it was immediately contested by the equally absolute claims of the Huguenot insistence on the rights of religious conscience. Its reprise by Thomas Hobbes strengthened the absolutism of the ruler, but this renewed absolutism was transferred to the people by Rousseau. The absolutist claims of sovereignty (however defined) were the source of a fruitful ambiguity, which make it a useful explanatory tool that can adapt to changing conditions. Political thought interacts with political history, clarifying and being clarified.

While the historical examples through which Dieter Grimm illustrates this fruitful ambiguity may at first be familiar to the philosopher or political theorist, their formulation in the framework of constitutional legal theory sharpens the contrasting judgments by situated actors. For example, the conceptual arguments justifying American independence were not sufficient to explain the transformation of thirteen newly sovereign states united by a constitution whose foundation is the unitary (if fictive) sovereign called "We the people."[1] That solution was not without ambiguity, as Grimm demonstrates through his analysis of the contrasting positions of John C. Calhoun and Daniel Webster concerning a state's right to "nullification" of federal laws. Another illustration of fruitful ambiguity that will be less familiar to the Anglo-American reader is found in Grimm's account of the constitution of the German

Reich after its unification under Bismarck in 1871. In this case the new united German "state" has to be distinguished from the sovereignty of those dominions that became its members in order to provide a juridical frame that could govern the new institutional reality.

These examples illustrate the fact that the concept of sovereignty has come to be associated with that of a constitution. A constitution has at once to preserve the sovereign but also to limit it because the sovereign power (be it the people or the states or the state) and the executive power cannot be identical. The independence of the one or the other power would create disorder or lead to tyranny. The constitution that articulates their relation thus becomes the locus of sovereignty. Constitutions of course are created to deal with specific circumstances and are to be judged accordingly. Grimm demonstrates the extraordinary plasticity and internal logic of the concept of sovereignty as it acquires the forms of popular sovereignty, national sovereignty, the sovereignty of the state, the locus of sovereignty in a federal state, and finally manifests what Grimm calls "latent sovereignty."[2] Although these forms of constitutional sovereignty present a historical sequence, Grimm does not claim that they describe an immanent teleology. It is significant that sovereignty becomes "latent" when the constitutional state has been fully realized in the Basic Law of contemporary Germany (which, Grimm notes, was not subject to popular ratification, as opposed to the Weimar constitution, which was so ratified).

Of course a state, a nation, a confederation, a people, or a government cannot be sovereign alone; that was the ultimate ground for the failure of the Westphalian system (although, as Grimm demonstrates, attempts were made to provide rules for relations among autonomous sovereigns). In the twentieth century more comprehensive attempts to make compatible internal and external sovereignty took the form of treaties that created international institutions of different types, such as the United Nations but also the Universal Declaration of Human Rights as well as such economic institutions as the World Trade Organization. The growth of the network of these diverse international institutions poses the question whether the twenty-first century will mark the era of "postsovereignty." At the very least, Dieter Grimm suggests, we can no longer speak of a world organized by a hierarchy of institutions; we live, rather, in a "heterarchy" that poses more questions than it offers answers.

When he turns finally to the relevance of the concept of sovereignty today, as both explanatory concept but also as a political reality, Dieter Grimm shows himself to be a generous and careful interpreter of opposing arguments that remain actual and contested. Indeed, the EU parliamentary elections of 2014 brought to power radical parties (mainly on the right side of the spectrum) that denounce the institutions of the union as antidemocratic. These results pose once again the question whether the European Union is a "postsovereign" political reality that opens new space for democratic life beyond the nation-state. Or does the practice of democratic self-determination still depend on the existence of a sovereign state? Dieter Grimm's concluding sentence affirms that "sovereignty today is also the protection of democracy." But his engaging study teaches us that the reach and the meaning of sovereignty can and will undergo further development.

Preface and Acknowledgments

This book is not intended as a history of sovereignty or the concept of sovereignty. For that, it would have had to be far more extensive. However, frequent encounters with ahistorical treatments of the concept of sovereignty strengthened my decision to write it. It should instead serve as a reminder of the contextual nature and the adaptability of the concept of sovereignty. To accomplish this, it is sufficient to consider some significant stages in its development. I see the book as helping to clarify the question whether, in the early twenty-first century, the concept of sovereignty still has an object in the real world and fulfills a function that justifies its continued use, or if the changes in recent decades have cut the ground out from under it. The basis of this text was a far shorter piece for *Traité international de droit constitutionnel,* published in Paris.

Professor Dick Howard accepted the book for publication in the Columbia Studies in Political Thought/Political History. The translation was made possible by a grant from the Börsenverein des deutschen Buchhandels. Belinda Cooper translated the text with remarkable sensitivity. Andrea Katz prepared French sources and quotations for the English-speaking reader where possible. Of particular help was the Library Service of the Wissenschaftskolleg zu Berlin (Institute for Advanced Study). To all I am greatly indebted.

SOVEREIGNTY

Sovereignty in a Time of
Changing Statehood

For centuries, sovereignty has been a key concept in political and legal discourse. This is not to say, however, that its meaning has always been obvious or that it has even remained the same. Its connection to political rule has been constant since the thirteenth century. But political systems changed so fundamentally in the ensuing eight hundred years that the concept of sovereignty could not remain unaffected. It was forced to adapt more than once to the great changes in the development of political rule. As a result, more than a few characteristics of the concept of sovereignty have changed their meaning over time, so that the continuing use of the term does not necessarily imply that its content remains the same.

Not only has the meaning of the term changed over time. Originating in France, it developed its increasing attractiveness, beginning in the late sixteenth century, outside its country of origin. There, however, it encountered greatly varied political situations and intellectual traditions. This, too, affected its meaning. Despite its great attractiveness, the concept could only be applied in different contexts if its meaning was altered. Thus just as *sovereignty* cannot claim a timeless meaning, it is not a concept that remains the same regardless of location. Instead, it can be assumed that its content also changes from country to country.

But, even at the same time and in the same place, the meaning of *sovereignty* has seldom been fixed. As a rule, competing interpretations have striven for primacy. The great debates about the legitimacy and shape of government are reflected in this terminological competition. The questions have almost always involved what sovereignty is and who holds it. The question of what it is includes, in particular, the subsidiary question whether sovereignty represents abstract or concrete, divisible or indivisible authority. The question of who holds it asks in particular the subsidiary question whether it belongs to an individual or a collective and whether its possession and exercise must be in the same hands or can be separated. These questions did not, however, extend to sovereignty in and of itself.

This has now changed. More recently, the question that has come to the fore is whether the concept of sovereignty still has a role to play. Unlike earlier questions, this one is aimed not at the substance but at the object of the term. It seems doubtful whether the object encompassed by the concept of sovereignty still exists. If it has disappeared, further use of the term would have lost its purpose. It would no longer have any value in explaining reality and would only continue as a figure of speech, camouflaging rather than illuminating actual relationships. This would suggest new changes in the area of political rule—this time, however, of such a radical nature that there would no longer be a reason to adapt the term.

This possibility cannot be ruled out. The concept of sovereignty did not possess from the very start the central role it has held until recently. It owes its central role to a very particular historical constellation and is thus not immune to loss of meaning if this constellation disappears. The key change was the religious schism of the sixteenth century. This pulled the rug out from under the medieval order and brought forth a new form of political rule, which differed from its predecessor by concentrating and augmenting the powers of the ruler while simultaneously limiting their reach territorially. It was Jean Bodin who added these characteristics to the concept of sovereignty and thus lent it new, extraordinarily potent significance.[1]

A political order that included these characteristics was soon understood to be a "state." State formation became the dominant theme of the era, and sovereignty the desideratum of all rulers. To the degree that state formation progressed, the universal Christian world order made room for particularist states existing side by side, which defined themselves by their claims to sovereignty and regulated their relations on that basis. Sovereignty thus gained an internal and an external dimension, which met, however, in the right of self-determination. Self-determination regarding the internal affairs of the state could only exist if the state was free from heteronomy in its external affairs.

It is these very requirements of sovereignty, however, that are currently undergoing a process of change. We recognize that statehood is eroding everywhere. The main cause of this is an increasing need for security and necessity for regulation, brought forth mainly by scientific and technological progress and its military and commercial uses. This places an increased burden upon the problem-solving capacities of territorially limited states as well as on traditional alliances of states. States have therefore proceeded to create supranational institutions to which they have transferred sovereign rights in order to cope with the growing number of transnational problems. These rights are now exercised by the supranational institutions with binding effect within states. The correspondence of public authority and state authority, which went hand in hand with the modern concept of sovereignty, is thus dissolving.

This is a change that, in its epochal significance, follows not far behind the emergence of the modern state in the sixteenth century and its transformation into the democratic constitutional state in the eighteenth century. For this reason, the current doubts about the value of the concept of sovereignty are also more plausible than the challenges and death notices from the great sovereignty deniers of the late nineteenth and early twentieth century such as Hugo Preuss, Léon Duguit, and Hans Kelsen.[2] Their attacks were directed at a particular concept of sovereignty, one that contradicted their understanding of law and state, but their interpretations would have been compatible with other concepts of sovereignty.

When these authors were formulating their theories, neither the United Nations nor the World Trade Organization existed, let alone the European Union. True, states are far from dissolving into these institutions. Even under altered conditions, states remain the political actors richest in powers and instruments of force. But no state today is sovereign in the traditional sense, which ruled out any form of external control. This is true to a particularly great extent for the member states of that unprecedented entity, the European Union, which has exploded the traditional dualism of a confederation of states and a federal state, possesses the authority to act in numerous areas of policy, and claims precedence for its decisions over national law. It is mainly due to the European Union that the question of sovereignty has been posed in a new way.

The answers vary. Sovereignty is defended by some, disputed by others, redefined by still others. Not all authors are aware of sovereignty's many possible meanings. Whether one accepts or denies the existence of an object that could sensibly be captured by the concept of sovereignty depends, under today's conditions, on what content one finds in the concept. So the old questions, such as that of the divisibility of sovereignty, retain their significance. Assertions about sovereignty are not made more persuasive by identifying the term with one interpretation, in ignorance of all the others, or by supposedly redefining it.

The dangers of thus identifying or redefining the concept can be avoided only if one understands the concept of sovereignty in its historical context. In his "General Theory of the State," Georg Jellinek began the chapter on sovereignty with this insight.[3] It requires, above all, taking into account the circumstances, ideas, and interests to which the various interpretations of sovereignty owe their origins and ascertaining the functions that the various concepts of sovereignty fulfill in their shifting constellations. Only then can we examine whether they will be able to endure even under current conditions or are so connected to the conditions of their emergence that they are no longer suited to the present.

This awareness must also guide the interpretation and application of legal texts. When constitutions, international treaties, and statutes use or presume the concept of sovereignty, they are also operating within this context and acting selectively toward it, wittingly or unwittingly. For this reason, in interpreting *sovereignty,* we must not allow individual pieces of the conceptual tradition to dominate the interpretation, to be held for the whole or for all that is possible, or even to be so ideologically freighted that certain conclusions seem to be logically unavoidable. Such a procedure always leads to contestable results.

In understanding the concept of sovereignty, it is helpful to compare not only time frames but also countries. The reason is that the great constitutional and, even more, international law principles and their interpretations are rarely the result of purely national developments. Instead, they frequently take shape during processes of transnational exchange. These varying influences do not necessarily lead, however, to transnational understandings. National variants develop, whose differences often go unnoticed because of similarities of terminology. In this respect as well, a comparative view is of great importance. Only in light of foreign developments can national peculiarities be recognized as such.

Insofar as constitutional and treaty texts employ the concept of sovereignty, however, an interpretation that undermines the concept's legal validity is not permissible. Even if one were to reach the conclusion that sovereignty had lost its relevance, the norm would not therefore become obsolete, as marriage law would become obsolete if no one married; for, unlike the concepts of marriage, art, the press, or a profession, which also tend not to be defined more precisely in constitutions, the concept of sovereignty does not refer to an actual object, but operates in the realm of imagination and ideas.[4] If raised to constitutional status, the idea that a state has to be sovereign must therefore be given a viable meaning. This can potentially force substantial conceptual readjustment.

Nondoctrinal disciplines such as political science, or the nondoctrinal branches of legal scholarship such as the theory of the state, are not subject to these pressures. Scholars in these areas might come to the conclusion that the concept of sovereignty, despite its recognition as positive law, has become irrelevant or at least has ceased to apply to the European Union. But, even then, one must ask whether its continued use is based on the persistence of scholarly discourse, which often leads concepts to outlive the objects they describe. In that case they contribute nothing more to understanding existing conditions, but fulfill only "rhetorical functions," as has been surmised of sovereignty.[5]

It is also possible—not for the first time in the history of the concept of sovereignty—that we must merely abandon certain, possibly deep-rooted, ideas of sovereignty because they no longer correspond to reality, while the concept itself retains substance and functions that cannot be replaced in other ways. In that case, new definitions would be necessary; not infrequently, though not always consciously, they will fall back upon older concepts of sovereignty. Finally, it is also possible that, aside from any functional purposes, the concept of sovereignty satisfies a deep-seated need to protect a society's political identity and self-determination and that this keeps it alive.[6]

B

Development and Function
of the Concept of Sovereignty

I

Bodin's Significance for the Concept of Sovereignty

I. *SOVEREIGNTY* BEFORE BODIN

Sovereignty is linked, like no other principle of politics or law, with the name of one author: Jean Bodin. Bodin did not invent the word, however; it already existed.[1] The expressions *sovereign* and *sovereignty* had been linked to political rule since the thirteenth century in France, where they first appeared a century earlier. In the beginning, they served to characterize concrete phenomena of significant height, such as mountains or towers. Somewhat later, they were also used to describe the power of God.[2] The reference to physical objects was soon lost. The application to God continued for a somewhat longer time. The term's use in connection with political rule became common.

In terms of rule, sovereignty described the highest, final decision-making authority, which lent its holder power over others. Those who had no lord above them in regard to such power and were not dependent on the consent of others were called sovereign. Possession and exercise of sovereignty were coextensive. The power to govern was always held by a person who also exercised it. This did not prevent him from using others to aid him in this exercise. However, these others, even when permitted to utilize instruments of power, were not themselves sovereign. Sovereignty was not based on the use of instruments of power, but only on the highest independent power of disposition. He who ultimately remained master of the exercise of power was sovereign.

Because, in the Middle Ages, such positions of power were not held by a single person, but were distributed territorially and functionally among many mutually independent holders, sovereignty could be linked only with individual powers. As a result, "sovereignty" described not an abstract but a concrete position of power, and many "sovereigns" coexisted on one and the same territory. "Sovereignty" was not a unified concept, but a plural one. Because it built upon individual powers, the characteristic of being sovereign did not suffer from the fact that its possessor was subordinate to a higher holder in regard to other powers. One could only be relatively, not absolutely, sovereign.

In this sense, the king was the primary sovereign, but not the only one, since he was not superior to the other holders of powers in all, or even most, regards. The characteristic of being sovereign in fact extended down to the barons. "Each baron is sovereign in his barony."[3] Even the holders of certain offices, such as offices at court, were considered sovereign if they were the final decision-making authorities within their spheres of responsibility. Institutions could also be termed sovereign. The term for the royal court in France was "the sovereign court of the Parliament of Paris" (*La court souveraine du parlement de Paris*). The president of the court of justice, too, was considered sovereign in regard to the judges subordinate to him.

The number of powers made no difference. The king might possess more powers or, as they had been called since the fourteenth century, sovereign rights than a count or baron. But this did not effect an increase in sovereignty. Sovereignty was not an aggregate concept. Even a single power of final decision making lent its possessor the characteristic of being sovereign. If one wished to describe the elevated status of the monarch among the many sovereigns, one used the word *seigneurie*. Although, in the course of the dispute between emperor and pope at the end of the fourteenth century, increasing reference was made to the *souveraineté* of the French king, this remained merely a collective term for certain powers that were his due.

It is true that the view is sometimes expressed among medievalists that the English and French kings had already, by the late thirteenth and early fourteenth centuries, attained a position of power that reflected the essential elements of Bodin's concept of sovereignty. In this view, reality preceded theory by 150 years. "Recognition of the kings' unique executive power came several generations before Bodin formulated his doctrine of sovereignty,"[4] and the later formulation of the concept merely reinforced an already long-initiated development. But the concept of "sovereignty" did not refer to this position before Bodin. *Seigneurie* could not be replaced by *souveraineté*.[5] And it was also distinguished from the later doctrine of sovereignty by its limitation to "executive power."

Conversely, the claim that the feudal Middle Ages was unfamiliar with sovereigns can only be maintained if one ignores the medieval use of *sovereign* and instead backdates Bodin's modern concept of sovereignty.[6] There was indeed no "final source of authority and jurisdiction"—Bodin's definition of *sovereign*—on the secular level. Nor could one have existed; that would have denied the status of God, from whose authority all powers of government were derived and to whose world order they belonged. One might argue about the relationship between worldly and religious power, emperor and pope, but not over the fact that both received their authority from God and were therefore not "final."

Furthermore, sovereignty did not refer to unlimited power. Concretely, in the Middle Ages its object was only temporal affairs. A holder of worldly powers of rule was sovereign. His power extended only to secular matters, even if these were divinely ordained. Spiritual matters were the responsibility of the Church and its officials. But these officials were not viewed as sovereign. This was also true of the pope, even though the *plenitudo potestatis* ascribed to him would later at times be interpreted as "sovereignty."[7] Where the limits were drawn might be up for dispute. There were constant arguments over this. But there was no dispute about the fact that limits existed and that they restricted the scope of sovereignty by withholding certain matters from it from the start.

But even in the temporal arena there was no unlimited right to rule. At times an absolute power (*puissance absolue*) is mentioned in connection with sovereignty, but it meant only sole responsibility and final decision-making power, not the freedom to use such power at will. Each power, instead, had a legal framework and a legal objective. It could only be exercised in conformity with legal guidelines. The holder of sovereign rights could not unilaterally change the conditions of its exercise. Resistance was permitted against a sovereign who overstepped these limits; under some circumstances it was even required. Any person could act as protector of objective law. *Absolu* did not mean *legibus solutus.*

The *leges* that regulated the power to rule were prescribed. Functionally, sovereignty did not include the right to autonomous lawmaking. The social order was established by God-given or natural law, but, in any case, not by man-made law. Political rule existed primarily to implement law or reestablish it when it was violated. Lawmaking was limited to making existing law more concrete, or at least it had to claim to be doing this. Ascertaining the law was most important. The function of finding the law antedated the function of making law. Thus the expression *sovereign* referred with particular frequency to the power of dispensing justice.

2. SOVEREIGNTY IN BODIN

The social relationships of the Middle Ages were reflected in this concept of sovereignty.[8] A separate system specializing in political rule had not yet developed. Instead, rule was usually practiced as an annex to a certain status, generally that of property owner. It was thus distributed among numerous holders, of which none possessed comprehensive, let alone absolute, powers to rule. It also referred not to a limited territory, but to persons, so that the inhabitants of an area could be subject to a variety of lords, depending on the respective powers they exercised. The system itself could not be changed by the ruler. It was perceived to be God-given and sacrosanct.

Because the concept of sovereignty reflected the conditions prevailing in the period of its emergence, it could not remain unaffected by the collapse of the medieval order in the wake of the religious schism and the emergence of a novel form of government, the modern state. Bodin's significance lies in the fact that he drew consequences for the notion of sovereignty from these changes. In so doing, he did not limit himself to the immediate occasion of his work; instead, he generalized the key conclusions he drew from these developments and underpinned them theoretically.[9] At the same time, the historical cause retained its significance for the specific way in which Bodin redefined the concept of sovereignty. Thus the context is important, both for Bodin's theory of sovereignty and for its later transformation.

The reason for Bodin's work was the wars of religion that swept France in the sixteenth century. The schism did not destroy the conviction that the world was ordered according to God's will and that humans, whether rulers or ruled, had to comport themselves according to that truth. But there was disagreement over what God's will was. This divided supporters of traditional belief from those wishing to free the faith from the falsifications of which they accused the Church of Rome. Both claimed divine truth for their interpretation and believed themselves justified in using violence to assert it. They were thus implacable foes.

Bodin was born in 1529 or 1530 into an already religiously divided world. The wars of religion began thirty years later, in 1562, when the crown abandoned its original tolerant course and backed the Catholic cause. Efforts by the French monarchy to make themselves absolute rulers had already started. Without breaking radically with the traditional order, they began to oppose, limit, or ignore the rights of the estates and the courts. At the same time, they strove, by fashioning their own apparatus of control, to free themselves from dependence on the estates. These efforts peaked around 1560, supported by a decidedly royalist literature that derived the monarch's omnipotence from French law.[10]

A new word soon appeared for this novel form of political rule, in which politics developed into an independent function related to a territory, with a concentration of power and a governing apparatus oriented toward its use: namely *state*. It was no longer used only in compound form—a state of something—but on its own. The chancellor of the absolutist regime, Michel de L'Hôpital, used it in the abstract form as early as 1562 in a speech before the Estates General. Bernard de Girard, no supporter of the royalists, called France a state in 1570. Bodin was also familiar with the expression; it frequently appears in his writings as a synonym for *republic*.[11]

However, other writers turned against these absolutist efforts and their supporters, emphasizing the limits of monarchical rule. The first work with which Bodin gained the attention of the scholarly world, *Methodus ad facilem historiarium cognitionem,* in 1566, can be viewed in this context. The St. Bartholomew's Day Massacre of 1572, in which he almost lost his life, exacerbated the disputes. The Huguenots referred to the right to resistance to justify their struggle against the crown. Bodin's immediate objective in his *Six Books of the Commonwealth* in 1576 was to refute that position. For him, sovereignty was the key concept in dealing with the situation.[12]

Still, both sides remained convinced that there could only be "one faith, one law, one king" (*une foi, une loi, un roi*). The parties' irreconcilability, however, led a group of authors to question this premise. They did not doubt that preserving the true faith and the unity of faith were important. But, in their view, these could not be taken so seriously as to jeopardize the existence of the polity. The polity took priority over the question of truth, about which agreement seemed impossible. These authors therefore strove for a solution to the conflict independent of religious truth—that is, a purely political solution—and were dismissively called "politicians" (*les politiques*) by their contemporaries.[13]

Bodin was one of them. In his view, a superior power was necessary to achieve the goal of restoring internal peace, one that could rise above the warring factions and force them into a secular order that would allow the opposing faiths to exist side by side, by turning faith into a private matter. From a historical perspective, this could only be done by the king, who, at the tip of the medieval feudal pyramid, had no lord above him and already possessed a large number of sovereign rights. The first condition was that he could consolidate the scattered sovereign rights in his hands and become independent of others in exercising them.

But that could not be the end of it. The ruler needed this wealth of powers not merely to end the war but also to create and implement a new, peaceful order. Therefore, and second, the power to make law was also necessary. Bodin called this expanded legal power "sovereignty." Because of the collapse of the medieval order and the dependence of domestic peace on a new order that left aside the issue of truth, this legislative power was, to Bodin, even the "principal mark of sovereign majesty" (*le point principal de la maiesté souveraine*). The most important characteristic of the sovereign is that he "makes law for the subject, abrogates law already made, and amends obsolete law."[14]

This law was not and could not be restricted to the temporal, if it were to fulfill its purpose. It applied to all matters important for establishing and maintaining domestic peace. No area of law could be reserved to the Church. Ecclesiastical sanctions could not be allowed to affect the worldly status of the individual.[15] It included the power to overturn existing law and abrogate customary law. The extension of public power to lawmaking also marked the birth of positive law. Law's validity was no longer based in divine will, but in the will of the sovereign. "The laws . . . proceed simply from his own free will."[16]

Sovereignty was now no longer what it had been in the Middle Ages. True, it continued to designate the highest level of independently exercised power. This characteristic was in fact what suggested applying the concept of sovereignty to the new situation. Freed from its relationship to discrete, concrete powers, the concept now described the complete possession of governing authority. It thus lost its concreteness and relativity. Sovereignty was now an abstract power that gained its changing content from the way it was handled by the ruler. He was also no longer relatively sovereign, compared to other holders of sovereign rights, but absolutely sovereign. Sovereignty was thus no longer a collective term for a bundle of powers. It now described a unity that was more than the sum of its parts.

To Bodin, unified sovereignty also required a single holder whom he could not imagine as anything but a concrete person or persons. From a historical perspective, only a king was conceivable, but Bodin did not settle theoretically on a monarch. He also saw the possibility of a collective of persons—the nobility or the people—as the holder of sovereignty. Only a division of sovereignty among several independent holders was ruled out. A number of holders would have made each dependent on the agreement of the others and thus unsovereign.[17] A "mixed government" did not meet the conditions Bodin placed on sovereignty. Sovereignty was indivisible. Partial sovereignty did not deserve the name.

In this way, possession and exercise remained in one place. The fact that others also had authority in addition to the ruler did not affect his sovereignty, as long as their authority was derived from the ruler and exercised at his behest. To Bodin, sovereignty was not identical with *puissance publique*. Rather, there were two types of *puissance publique*: "One is the sovereign right which is absolute, unlimited, and above the law, the magistrates and all citizens. The other is legal right, subject to the laws and the sovereign. This is proper to the magistrate, and those who have extraordinary powers conferred on them by commission. These persons can exercise the right only until their office is revoked or their commission expired."[18] Earlier powers could thus continue to be exercised under the new conditions, but not on one's own authority and under one's own conditions.

Bodin did not, however, go so far as to define sovereignty as unlimited power. This was particularly clear where lawmaking was concerned. The right to legislate was the most important and sole right of the sovereign. However, the sovereign only exercised his legislative power lawfully if he did so in conformity with the "constitutional laws of the realm," which included the succession and the inalienability of crown lands. Furthermore, the sovereign was bound by the "law of God and of nature," which was, however, universalized and thus removed from the Church's right of interpretation, "deconfessionalized."[19] Bodin's sovereign was above the law, but not above justice. He was not yet absolute, in the absolutist sense. He was even denied access to private property and he still needed the consent of the estates to collect taxes.[20]

The limitations on the right to make law could not, however, be enforced against the will of the sovereign. Bodin declared laws that did not adhere to these conditions to be "unjust and dishonorable."[21] Yet, if one might appeal against a law, and if there were a body that could declare it invalid and abrogate it, the prince would no longer be sovereign. A right of resistance against unlawful rule was unacceptable to Bodin, because it would place into question the overriding value of domestic peace. He was decisively opposed to the Huguenot standpoint, but allowed subjects to remonstrate and even to refuse to obey obviously unlawful laws in concrete situations.

3. SOVEREIGNTY AFTER BODIN

In 1576 there was no country in which the legal position of the ruler corresponded to Bodin's concept of sovereignty. Bodin's achievement would be lessened if one were to assume that he merely gave a name to an altered reality.[22] He did not, it is true, develop his doctrine out of nothing; he was able to build upon the strengthening of the French king that had begun earlier, and could take up trends of the day that were already recognizable in politics and literature, but he transformed them into a novel concept that would make it possible to achieve the purposes of political rule under the new conditions of plurality of religious belief. Thus his writings did not primarily explain the status quo, but outlined a prospective theory.

The effects of this theory cannot be overstated. Within five years, nine editions of Bodin's work had been published in France. By the first third of the seventeenth century, more than twenty editions had been issued in

French, and around ten in Latin. It was published in Italian translation in 1588, in Spanish in 1590, in German in 1592, and in English in 1606.[23] Its effects were not confined to the scholarly world. Sovereignty became the model for European princes. Their efforts to achieve sovereignty triggered a process of change in political rule from which the state emerged as a new form of government—though it would vary from country to country and would nowhere reach completion until the end of the *ancien régime*.

State and *sovereignty* distinguished the new epoch from the Middle Ages. While the concept of sovereignty was an old one that now described something new, the *state* was new not only in substance but as a concept. A *medieval state* existed only in the writings of a few historians.[24] The two terms were closely related. One spoke of sovereignty when a ruler was able to disarm the intermediate powers and consolidate scattered sovereignty rights into a unified public authority. A polity that achieved this was considered a state. Public authority and state authority thus became one. The holder of this authority, the sovereign, was the monarch.

France came closest to this model, beginning with Henry IV and continuing with Armand-Jean du Plessis, duc de Richelieu. The monarchy was largely able to avoid giving the estates a say in government and became independent of their services through a powerful state bureaucracy. After 1614 the Estates General did not meet again until 1789. But the feudal system, which granted rights of rule to the lords, guilds, and other corporations, was left untouched, and these rights prevented the ruler from exercising direct power over all inhabitants. Peasants, in particular, remained the subjects of their lords and were also subject to their judicial power. The newly acquired legislative power of the sovereign was used quite frequently, but not yet in a systematic way.

In Germany the princes of the larger territories, especially Prussia and Austria, succeeded in establishing a similar domestic position as the king in France. For the great majority of German princes, however, this was not the case. Behind absolutist facades, the traditional system survived. Furthermore, all the territories, as members of the Holy Roman Empire, remained at least partially subject to the supreme power of the emperor, who, though he made no attempt to turn the Reich into a sovereign state, did prevent the local princes from enjoying complete sovereignty because of the empire's continuing authority over them.

In England, meanwhile, the feudal system gradually declined, without ever being formally abolished. But the Stuarts' attempts in the seventeenth century to move England closer to an absolute monarchy on the continental model failed due to the combined resistance of the aristocracy and the bourgeoisie. In the Glorious Revolution of 1688, which, unlike the revolutions of the eighteenth century, aimed not to establish a new order but to defend the old one, Parliament was able not only to consolidate but to expand its political rights. England became a "mixed government," consisting of the king, the House of Lords, and the House of Commons, and thus could not be considered sovereign, according to Bodin's concept of sovereignty.

On the conceptual level, this led to constant adaptation of Bodin's definitions to fit existing conditions. But radicalizations also emerged, as well as alternative concepts lacking any pragmatism. In France, but elsewhere too, one could find attempts by jurists to bridge the gap between aspiration and reality by maintaining that the sovereign rights remaining with the estates and corporations had been delegated by the princes, which implied the power to claim those rights for themselves—the very power the holders of these rights denied. Others reduced the concept to the monarch's sole decision-making power and the irreversibility of his decisions in his spheres of authority, but quietly abandoned the characteristic of possession of complete public authority.

In England monarchs after James I attempted, with theoretical support especially from Robert Filmer, and with reference to Bodin, to raise the bundle of privileges that was their due to the level of sovereignty.[25] Edward Coke, in contrast, argued that the sovereign power of the king was not a "parliamentary word." The Parliament, in his view, was in a position to "maketh, enlargeth, abrogateth, repealeth, and riviveth laws, statutes, acts, ordinances, concerning matters ecclesiastical, criminal, canon, civil, marital, maritime, and the rest."[26] In the second half of the seventeenth century, and definitely after 1688, the view had taken hold that sovereignty belonged to the "King in Parliament"—that is, to three independent institutions that together represented the whole.

In Germany the constitutional discourse after 1600 fell under the spell of Bodin's concept of sovereignty, although it was apparent that his core principle, the indivisibility of sovereignty, did not fit the conditions of the Reich.[27] The Reich possessed a mixed constitution that most authors believed was preferable to purer forms of government. Bodin himself, however, interpreted the Reich constitution to place sovereignty in the hands of the Reich estates and therefore classified the Reich not as a monarchy but as an aristocracy.[28] Generally, however, there is no question where he believed sovereignty to be best situated: in the hands of the monarch.

This placed German jurists in an ambivalent position. The imperial side rejected Bodin's classification of the Reich, but took his theories as a basis to prove that the Kaiser possessed undivided sovereignty.[29] Supporters of the Reich estates dismissed Bodin's preference for monarchical sovereignty, but also used his theories to show that undivided sovereignty was the right of the Reich estates, while the Kaiser was merely the highest organ of the Reich.[30] In the end, the difference was bridged with a formula that took up Bodin's Latin translation of *souveraineté* as *majestas,* by ascribing *majestas realis* to the Reich and *majestas personalis* to the Kaiser.

These examples confirm the effect of Bodin's concept of sovereignty on his contemporaries. Sovereignty had to be invoked even when powers had not yet been concentrated into a unified public authority or, as in the Reich, this could not even be attempted. The result was that the divisibility of sovereignty, which Bodin had rejected, continued to run through discussions on sovereignty. The idea was propped up, if reluctantly (*irregularis*), by such leading authorities as Hugo Grotius, whose Dutch experience could not be reconciled with the postulate of unified sovereignty, and Samuel Pufendorf, who did not succeed in describing the Reich using Bodin's categories.[31]

While Bodin's concept of sovereignty was watered down to adapt it to the respective realities, an alternative concept of sovereignty was forming in a campaign against the very movement set in motion by Bodin. It was the Huguenot authors who, following St. Bartholomew's Day, attempted to justify their resistance to the crown theoretically by resorting to earlier scholastic concepts of the contractual legitimacy of secular rule. In this view, a people did not surrender its original sovereignty through the social contract, but merely transferred the right to exercise this sovereignty to the monarch. This transfer was conditional.

The king's failure to live up to the contract justified resistance—for the monarchomachs, even his murder.

The result was, as Quentin Skinner says, "a fully developed political theory of revolution, founded on a recognizable modern, secularized thesis about the natural rights and original sovereignty of the people," which was most radically advocated by George Buchanan in Scotland and Johannes Althusius in Germany.[32] For the Calvinist theoreticians, however, the significance of popular sovereignty amounted to little more than a justification of resistance. With its help, the monarch would be prevented from ignoring the estates and magistrates, viewed as representatives of the popular sovereign, but this would not create a system of popular rule. Yet the idea of the contract brought the people into play and with them the necessity of distinguishing between possessing and exercising sovereignty.

Not even Thomas Hobbes could escape these consequences in his book *Leviathan,* which appeared seventy-five years after Bodin's *Six Books* and took the concept of sovereignty to its farthest limits. Responding to the English wars of religion, he, like Bodin, assumed that restoring domestic peace required an omnipotent and irresistible authority. However, he agreed with the Calvinists that the legitimation of such an authority could only emanate from the people, whom he therefore granted a primordial freedom in shaping the political system. But the value of security, which overrode all else in the wake of the civil war, was for him worth the price of freedom. Unlike the Calvinists, he therefore assumed that, in the social contract, individuals surrendered all natural rights to the ruler and thus provided him with complete sovereignty.

Hobbes's twelve attributes of sovereignty show the extent to which sovereignty was strengthened in his work.[33] The sovereign, it is true, does not possess sovereignty originally but gains it through a "covenant" among the individuals who join to form the state. But they cannot change this covenant without the agreement of the sovereign. Because they have surrendered their natural rights to the sovereign completely and unconditionally, no one can dissolve the covenant due to a violation of rights by the ruler. Anyone who does not agree to the covenant can be destroyed if he does not submit. Unlawful behavior by the sovereign is inconceivable. Resisting him is as out of the question as punishing him.

The following six elements of sovereignty described the functions that only the sovereign possessed: legislation, adjudication, making war and peace, allocating offices, reward and punishment, assigning ranks and honors. These powers were "indivisible, and inseparably annexed to the Sovereignty." Hobbes countered the objection that, in such a system, the situation of subjects is "very miserable" with the argument that only sovereignty thus understood could guarantee the security of the subjects and that it was therefore, on balance, rationally preferable to the alternative of civil war.[34]

Even if the state is nothing without the almighty sovereign, Hobbes was not interested, as he emphasized in his preface, in the individual sovereign, but in the supra-individual state. A clearer distinction is made between the two than was previously the case.[35] The person to whom the rights of individuals are transferred is not directly the natural person of the ruler, but the artificial, legal person of the state. This only becomes capable of action, however, because it has a representative, in the form of the natural person of the ruler. Because, to Hobbes, he is omnipotent, the distinction between the two persons has no practical consequences and is thus often ignored by interpreters of Hobbes.

Hobbes's intensification of sovereignty marked not only a theoretical high point but also a turning point. Like Bodin's doctrine, it emerged under conditions of religious civil war; however, it was free of any of the pragmatic considerations that could still be found in Bodin's works and could only remain plausible as long as the existential threat to life and limb was perceived as a real danger. The more successfully the sovereign state carried out its function of pacification, which necessitated a concentration of power in the hands of the ruler, the more questionable this unlimited power became. Thus the question of legitimacy was posed anew.

Only one generation after Hobbes, John Locke, in his *Two Treatises*—addressed less to Hobbes than to Filmer—derived the purpose of the state not from the value of security but from that of individual freedom. Insecurity in the state of nature was the reason for the transition to civil society. But, to fulfill its purpose of protection, the state no longer needed all of the individual's natural freedoms. Only the right to self-help had to be transferred. Therefore Locke purposely called the most important state authority, the legislature, not "sovereign" but "supreme." It was only the "trustee" of the people, which retained ultimate power and could put it to use if the parliament departed from the state's purpose of protecting freedom.[36]

In the second half of the eighteenth century, the natural law theories of the social contract began to be filled with expanding catalogues of human rights that were superordinate to the state.[37] These theories were aimed not at sovereignty as such but at the identification of sovereignty with unlimited power. The subjection of the individual to political authority was no longer justified by security alone, but also by the security of a free society that was no longer fundamentally threatened by civil war, though occasionally by aggression from without and lawbreakers from within. For this reason, too, a free society needed a powerful state authority, but it could do without an omnipotent one.

One hundred years after Hobbes, it was Jean-Jacques Rousseau who finally integrated the various sovereignty traditions into a discrete concept. He summarized his goal in the famous words "To find a form of association that may defend and protect with the whole force of the community the person and property of every associate, and by means of which each, joining together with all, may nevertheless obey only himself, and remain as free as before."[38] The solution Rousseau offered was that the people did not merely enthrone the sovereign, but were themselves sovereign, and remained so even after conclusion of the social contract. "Sovereignty cannot be represented."[39] As the sovereign, they are omnipotent, but since sovereignty does not devolve upon a representative, the danger of heteronomy is eliminated.

We cannot speak of a linear development of the sovereignty concept after Bodin, let alone of a uniform concept of sovereignty. Given the various stages of development of the European states reflected in the theories, this would be an unrealistic expectation. However, it would be equally incorrect to confuse the multiplicity of concepts with arbitrariness. Rather, the developments now definitively eliminated some of the pre-Bodin uses of the word. To the extent that the idea was shaped by a state characterized by its concentration of power, "sovereignty" could no longer refer to discrete, concrete powers in the hands of individuals.

Instead, the concept bundled the numerous concrete powers into an abstract public authority.

Public authority tended to have one subject as its holder. But even where constitutional relations suggested divisibility of sovereignty, for example in a federal entity such as an empire or a "mixed government" as in England, this division differed fundamentally from the medieval dispersal of numerous powers among a large number of independent holders. Further, the more one abstracted from the person of the ruler as holder, the more unavoidable became the distinction between possessing and exercising sovereignty. Also, the question of limitations no longer referred to the extent of discrete, concrete powers, but to the public authority itself, from the perspective of state purpose.

Sovereignty in the
Constitutional State

I. POPULAR SOVEREIGNTY

With the exception of Emer de Vattel, none of the authors who raised the question of the limits on state power or developed the concept of popular sovereignty derived the necessity of a constitution from these premises.[1] The contract theory mainly served as a test of the legitimacy of a political system. This test was met if the system could be imagined as having been voluntarily agreed upon by rational human beings. The idea of a legal document that established, rather than merely modifying, government and that comprehensively regulated the establishment and exercise of power was not part of this. Nor would this idea have been effective without the revolutionary break with hereditary rule and the resulting power vacuum.[2]

But when the constitution, in the modern sense, emerged from the two great revolutions of the late eighteenth century, the American and the French, popular sovereignty played a crucial role. Gordon Wood, one of the greatest experts on the American Revolution, where constitutionalism began, even called sovereignty "the single most important abstraction of politics in the entire Revolutionary period."[3] This proved to be true both for the revolution itself and for the founding of the United States of America with the adoption of the Constitution in 1787, which brought the revolutionary epoch to an end.

The dispute between the American colonies and the English motherland, that would end in independence was triggered by the special tariffs imposed on the colonists by the English Parliament through the Stamp Act of 1765. The colonists considered these incompatible with the rights of Englishmen, which were owed as much to them as to the inhabitants of the motherland. Without fundamentally questioning the authority of the London Parliament, they insisted on recognition of the principle of "no taxation without representation." They pointed out that they were only able to elect colonial parliaments, but could not send representatives to Westminster and thus were not represented in the decision-making body.

The colonists were not persuaded by London's response that they were represented virtually and pointed out the weaknesses of that argument. The English then shifted the discussion to the issue of sovereignty. Every society, they argued, had to have a final, supreme authority limited only by the laws of nature. Such a sovereign power was "the primary and essential condition of all political society" and needed no legitimation through representatives.[4] The compromises proposed by the colonists, with which they hoped to avoid a rift with the motherland, seemed to the English to lead to a division of sovereignty that would contradict the concept itself. The taxation debate thus turned into a question of preserving sovereignty that allowed for no compromise.

The colonists themselves ultimately realized this when William Blackstone, in his *Commentaries on the Laws of England,* which quickly gained popularity in America, confirmed the necessity of a "supreme, irresistible, uncontrolled authority, in which the *jura summi imperii,* or the sovereign rights reside."[5] Under these conditions, however, two parliaments could not claim authority over the same territory. Forced to make a choice, the colonists decided in favor of their own parliaments and claimed the right of "a free and exclusive power of legislation in their several provincial legislatures." When this was denied to them by English law, they constituted themselves—based on the "self-evident truths" of natural law—as "free and independent states."[6]

Thus sovereignty was transferred to the parliaments of the former colonies, now states, but without a king or upper house; for an American monarchy was out of the question, and feudal society never took hold in the colonies. If not for the way in which these parliaments then used their newly won sovereignty, there would have been no founding of the United States, ten years after the Declaration of Independence, and no redefinition of sovereignty as it emerged from the constitutional debate in Philadelphia. Sovereignty was once again crucial for this second stage in the revolutionary process.[7]

The former colonists had already decided during the dispute with the motherland to found a confederation called the United States of America. But this did not include surrendering their newly won sovereignty. The

Americans found confirmation in Vattel's statement that independent states could unite in a permanent confederation without sacrificing their character as states or their sovereignty.[8] Thus the question of the divisibility of sovereignty did not arise. The confederation was viewed as a union under the law of nations; its legal basis, the Articles of Confederation of 1781, was considered an international treaty. It began with the sentence: "Each state retains its sovereignty."

Yet it was precisely this individual state sovereignty that soon caused concern, due to the American version of parliamentary sovereignty, which lacked the moderating elements of English parliamentarianism. The brief history of postcolonial parliamentarianism was a history of arrogance on the part of the deputies, abuse of power, suppression of political opponents, broken treaties and failure to fulfill obligations, self-enrichment by deputies and betrayal of the common welfare. This explains the demand that the confederation be strengthened, once the individual state parliaments could no longer be trusted to make their own improvements.[9]

Yet the Federal Convention, charged with revising the Articles of Confederation, had no mandate to change the legal nature of the confederation and its legal basis, the articles. It was not intended as a constituent assembly.[10] Nevertheless, in its discussions the conviction quickly prevailed that the failures of the existing order could only be overcome by strengthening the confederation at the expense of the independence of the individual states. This led to a renewed debate on sovereignty, in which, however, the emphasis on the divisibility of sovereignty, which had taken primacy in the battle for independence, was shifted to a question of who held sovereignty.[11]

In resolving this question, it was of considerable importance that the parliaments, in their few years of independence, had forfeited their claims to sovereignty. It is true that self-government, about which the colonists had fought the war of independence, could not be imagined without a parliament. But a sovereign parliament did not meet the expectations associated with self-government. Therefore, the parliament's popular mandate took on a more prominent role. In the Federalist Papers, Alexander Hamilton compared this with the relationship between principal and agent, master and servant.[12] In this way a solution was provided to the question of who held sovereignty that was not available to England: popular sovereignty.

Until then, the people had acted as the entity that elected parliaments, but their decision-making power did not go beyond the vote. Now the question became one of perpetuating the supreme authority of the people and viewing the parliament as an organ of the people. In this way, the people remained present as the principal authority—unlike the people in social contract theory—and could demand accountability regarding the way in which the function was exercised. The constitution existed in order to regulate the details of the relationship between principal and agent. It could thus emanate only from the people and, in order to preserve popular sovereignty, had to be ranked above any organs and acts of the state.

This, however, resolved only one of the two problems—overcoming parliamentary sovereignty. The second involved curbing the autonomy of the individual states for the benefit of the United States. To do so, the latter had to be empowered to make decisions that were binding on the individual states. This could only succeed if the confederation were transformed into a state and its legal basis into a constitution. The obstacle to this was sovereignty. The individual states were unquestionably sovereign and had no interest in surrendering that status. However, the elevation of the confederation meant that it would gain power over the individual states. The question was how to reconcile the two.

James Madison, the leading mind at the convention, at first considered an "aggregate" or "coequal" sovereignty to be conceivable.[13] But the indivisibility doctrine, which had already dominated the revolutionary years, again asserted itself in opposition. On this point, federalists and antifederalists agreed. Once again, no middle way was available. A solution was offered in the form of a transfer of sovereignty from the people of the individual states to the people of the United States. "Madison was inventing a sovereign American people to overcome the sovereign states."[14] Neither the organs of the states nor those of the United States were sovereign; nor were the individual states or the United States sovereign. The American people alone were sovereign—in the view of the majority.[15]

The creation of a constitution, which was not part of the convention's mandate, had to then be legitimized by an act of the American people, which would take place in the existing entities, the individual states. However, in the majority view, the voters would not be called upon to vote as the people of individual states on their respective states' ratification of an international treaty, but as the American people on the adoption of their constitution.[16] The introductory words of the new Constitution do not reveal their full meaning if the quote ends, as is often the case, after the third word. "We the People of the United States" was revolutionary in a dual sense: "We the People" rather than "We the Government," and "We the People" rather than "We the States."

2. NATIONAL SOVEREIGNTY

The French Revolution had different opponents and different goals than the American Revolution. While the American Revolution was directed outwardly and waged for self-government vis-à-vis an empire, the French Revolution was directed inwardly and waged primarily for a fundamental change in the domestic social order. Only when this goal proved unattainable within the framework of the existing political system did the efforts broaden to include the overthrow of that system. This overthrow was not at first aimed at the monarchy, but at the legitimating basis of the monarchy's authority, which supported the traditional social order of the *ancien régime*: monarchical sovereignty.

The break with monarchical sovereignty did not, however, mark a break with sovereignty in general. In face of the enormous task of transforming the entire order according to the guiding principles of freedom and equality of the individual, sovereignty in France was instead practically a requirement for the success of the revolution—in contrast with America, where there was no need for a fundamental transformation of the legal order. It was thus the revolution that completed sovereignty on the night of August 4, 1789, by eliminating all existing intermediate powers and uniting the remaining prerogatives with the state's powers in a unified public authority.

As in America, natural law theories guided action at the moment of the revolutionary break with traditional rule and the resulting necessity of a new political order. This meant that sovereignty was transferred from the monarch to the people.[17] As in America, however, it was also clear that the people could not rule themselves. Contrary to Rousseau's view, public authority had to be entrusted to representatives of the people. Therefore, Title III, article 2 of the Constitution of 1791 provided that "the nation, from which alone all powers emanate, may exercise such powers only by delegation. The French Constitution is representative."

However, this concept contained a danger for sovereignty that Rousseau had hoped to avoid. It could not be ruled out that these representatives would deviate from the interests of the sovereign and use their power for reasons other than those intended by their masters.[18] This problem—a result of transferring sovereignty to the people when they could not exercise it themselves—would be resolved, as in America, by the constitution. In the constitution, the people, as sovereign, established binding legal conditions under which their representatives could exercise the power entrusted to them. Only on this basis, and within the limits set by it, would people be appointed to exercise power.

Exercise of public authority at the behest of the sovereign, which is not itself able to act, is thus the key to understanding this system. What the fathers of the American Constitution had described more metaphorically as the relationship between principal and agent, master and servant, was conceived of in France by Emmanuel Joseph Sieyes as a fundamental theoretical distinction between *pouvoir constituant* and *pouvoir constitué*.[19] The constituent power lay entirely with the people. It was not transferrable; popular sovereignty was realized through it. The people were free to choose how to use it. Even self-limitation was deemed incompatible with sovereignty. The restrictions created by the constituent power applied only to the representatives.

But the enactment of the constitution was also the end of the constituent power. It established the rules for political decision making. The decisions themselves were the job of the constituted power, which had, however, to act within the bounds of the powers transferred to it. From the start, its powers were limited. In particular, it could not arbitrarily change the conditions of its operation. As Sieyes clearly discerned, the primacy of the constitution, which flowed from the distinction between *pouvoir constituant* and *pouvoir constitué*, was an essential aspect of the constitution. Without primacy, it could not fulfill its function of binding the public authority to the prescriptions of the sovereign.

The most important means of limiting the constituted power were, as in America, basic rights and separation of powers. Constitutions that lacked these did not deserve the name. "Any society in which no provision is made for guaranteeing rights or for the separation of powers, has no Constitution," as laid out in article 16 of the declaration. Sovereignty was not only "imprescriptible and inalienable," it was "one and indivisible." Yet separation of powers did not contradict the indivisibility of sovereignty. Because it only affected the constituted power, which possessed no sovereignty but merely exercised public authority at the behest of the sovereign, it took place below the level of sovereignty and did not affect it.

At the same time, the separation between possessing and exercising power prevented the monarchy from contradicting popular sovereignty. The monarch also had to accept a change in his status. He was no longer the ruler by his own or divine right, but received his position and powers from a constitution prescribed by the people. "The representatives," read Title III, article 2 of the Constitution of 1791, "are the legislative body and the King." The king was a representative, appointed by the constitution, of the now sovereign people, as were the deputies of the *corps législative;* unlike them, however, he was not elected and was thus inferior to them.

The postrevolutionary sovereignty debate was long influenced by the revolution.[20] On the one hand, constitutionalism was one of the achievements that was not to be surrendered. On the other hand, popular sovereignty was now connected with the excesses of the revolution, which were not to be repeated. The return to monarchical sovereignty after the fall of Napoleon was thus only conceivable in the guise of constitutionalism. But it could certainly not be identical to prerevolutionary sovereignty. Constitutional rule is limited rule. The difference was overcome through the formulation that the monarch was the sole holder of sovereignty, but that he subjected himself to the constitution in its exercise.

The restoration did not last long, however. The solution to the problem was thereafter sought in other ways. The early liberals of the nineteenth century did not begin with the question of who held sovereignty, since they did not contest the people's right to it; instead, they again attempted to introduce substantive limits to sovereignty, as had the constitutional doctrines of the second half of the eighteenth century, though not the doctrine of *pouvoir constituant*. Benjamin Constant harked back to the idea of limited sovereignty when he said, "Sovereignty has only a limited and relative existence. At the point where independence and individual existence begin, the jurisdiction of sovereignty ends."[21]

However, a very different attempt was crucial to later developments; in this form, it had no equivalent outside France. It goes back to a terminological ambivalence that had already appeared in the first constitution. Although the deputies to the National Assembly had called themselves Representatives of the French People when the declaration was adopted in 1789, in article 3 they declared not the people but the nation to be the bearer of sovereignty. This was also the case in the Constitution of 1791. Title III, article 1 stated in regard to sovereignty, "It appertains to the nation." In determining what did not comport with this, however, the people once again appeared: "No section of the people nor any individual may assume the exercise thereof."

The king's attempt to flee in 1792 brought not only the monarchy but also the Constitution of 1791 to a rapid end. The Republican Constitution of 1793 no longer limited sovereignty to the act of constitution making. Departing from the purely representative principle of the Constitution of 1791, article 2 prescribed that the French people, "for the exercise of their sovereignty," were to be divided into primary assemblies and cantons, and article 29 granted them legislative powers. Above all, however, in connection with sovereignty, the constitution no longer spoke of the nation, but only of the people. In article 7 they were defined as the "whole mass of French citizens," a formulation that returned in the less democratic Constitution of the Year III.

The difference between nation and people as bearers of sovereignty would from then on dominate the French debate on sovereignty, long before Raymond Carré de Malberg gave it its classic expression.[22] *Souveraineté du people* (popular sovereignty) was in this view a concrete sovereignty, referring to the totality of living individuals, while *souveraineté de la nation* (national sovereignty) was an abstract sovereignty, referring to a collective subject across time made up of present and past generations. The former was realistic, the latter idealized; the former was individualistic and democratic, the latter organic and representative; the former transferred the sovereignty of the monarch to the people, while the second created an entirely new concept of sovereignty.

The distinction did not remain purely theoretical. Since the *souveraineté du peuple* was held responsible for the excesses of the revolution, while *souveraineté nationale* was considered protection from those excesses, the distinction led to practical consequences. Bridging the gap was the fact that the intergenerational nation was not capable of forming a common will, but a people composed of individuals was. Thus in France the constitutional debates on plebiscitary or representative democracy, census suffrage or universal suffrage, imperative or free mandate, which also took place in other countries, were treated as abstract debates about the concept of sovereignty in the constitution.

In Carré de Malberg's theory the sovereignty question ultimately became a question of constitutional amendment.[23] There was no longer a place for sovereignty in his strict legal positivism. If the state is the exclusive source of law, its founding cannot be a legal act. The same is true of the constitution. It creates the right to make law in the first place and cannot therefore regulate its own creation. "From this it follows that the initial formation of the state, as well as its first organization, cannot be considered but as a pure fact that does not lend itself to any legal classification, as this fact is not governed by principles of law."[24]

Once the state is founded and the constitution enters into force, the collective can exercise its will and its power only on the basis of specific rules, in specific forms, and through specific bodies, which are established in advance by the constitution. Before the state and the constitution, there is only actual power. In the state there are only legally based and limited powers. This is also true of the constituent power; from a legal perspective, it may only appear as the power that amends the constitution. As such, however, it is created by the constitution and bound by its provisions. Strictly speaking, for Carré de Malberg there was no "constituting body" (*organe constituant*). "Within the state, there are only constituted bodies."[25]

Carré de Malberg himself asks how this harmonizes with popular sovereignty. Since he regards sovereignty as a legal status, there is no sovereignty prior to the state or after a revolution. "It comes down to a question of fact and ceases to be a question of law."[26] At that moment, the people have no constituent authority. This authority is in the hands of "the most powerful."[27] As soon as the constitution has entered into force, no further recourse to the people is necessary. Changing the constitution is the job of the bodies provided for by the constitution. Popular sovereignty can only express itself through these bodies. It consists of "the power which belongs to the nation to express and impose its will through its regular bodies."[28]

The body responsible for amending the constitution is determined by the constitution. Carré de Malberg believed, however, that the principle of *souveraineté nationale*, in contrast to *souveraineté populaire*, "entails, as a necessary consequence, the separation of the *pouvoir constituant*."[29] The normal legislature may not amend the constitution, while the amending authority cannot change the laws. It seems doubtful that this can be reconciled with a purely positivist legal view. However, it is even more doubtful that Carré de Malberg's assumption that all the French constitutions, with the exception of the Constitution of the Year III, were the result of national sovereignty is justified.

This is doubtful for two reasons. First of all, the constitutions after Year III no longer clearly defined the bearers of sovereignty. Only in the short-lived revolutionary constitution of 1848 did the word again appear. The legal consequences derived from the concept of sovereignty thus no longer had a textual basis. Second, it seems quite doubtful that the claimed distinction was really laid out in the various revolutionary constitutions. The constitutional debates instead conveyed the impression that the expressions *nation* and *peuple* were used synonymously or were at least unaffected by the meanings later ascribed to them.[30]

Only in the postwar constitutions of 1946 and 1958 did the contradiction seem to be overcome. Both stated that *national* sovereignty lies with the *people*. In the constitutional literature, too, the contradiction began to lessen.[31] The consequences connected with it were no longer seen to be the logical result of the choice of words in the constitution. Nor did the Constitutional Council insist on the distinction. It refused to review the constitutionality of laws adopted by *popular* referendum, as they were the direct expression of *national* sovereignty.[32] Whether the people act here as the *pouvoir constituant* or only as the constitutionally bound *pouvoir constitué* is a different question.

3. STATE SOVEREIGNTY

Compared with America and France, Germany represents a special case that can for this very reason shed a different light on sovereignty.[33] No revolution took place in Germany around the end of the eighteenth and beginning of the nineteenth century to end monarchical sovereignty. Rather, the princes of the German territories gained full sovereignty after the dissolution of the Holy Roman Empire in 1806, though in some cases only under Napoleon's protectorate. The establishment of the German Confederation after the fall of Napoleon in 1815 did nothing to change this. Quite the contrary, the confederation saw itself as the "international union of sovereign German princes and free cities, to preserve the independence and inviolability of the states joined in the confederation."[34]

Even without a revolution, however, numerous princes began to enact constitutions in the early nineteenth century, though less out of constitutional convictions than out of an interest in preserving their own dynasties. In some cases revolts encouraged this willingness. But all the constitutions were voluntarily granted by the monarchs. The way in which they were created was not without repercussions for the issue of sovereignty. None of the monarchs was willing to abandon his sovereignty; yet, in taking the step toward a constitution, each one had to accept constitutional limitations on his powers through basic rights and the right of parliamentary assemblies to participate in lawmaking. The monarchs' authority was no longer unrestricted.

The tensions thus created between sovereignty and constitutional boundaries could not be resolved in the same way as in America or France. The road to popular sovereignty taken by those countries was not open to Germany. Article 13 of the Confederate Act did promise "constitutions of the estates" (*Landständische Verfassungen*) in all member states. But they were supposed to be a dam against popular sovereignty. The Final Act of the Congress of Vienna guaranteed monarchical sovereignty in article 57. The German Confederation was not least a defensive union against the threat of democratic constitutions. The use of force was permitted in order to put down attempted revolts in the member states that might threaten monarchical sovereignty.

These tensions would be resolved using the same formula that the restoration in France had already permitted to reconcile restoration of the monarchy with constitutionalism. The monarch was considered the sole bearer of sovereignty. In exercising it, however, he voluntarily bound himself to the provisions of the constitution. Article 57 of the Final Act of the Congress of Vienna gave expression to this formula.[35] Whereas in France the arrangement lasted only a relatively short time during the restoration period, in Germany it would determine the situation over the long term. It formed the basis of German constitutionalism until the fall of the monarchy at the end of World War I and the enactment of the Weimar Constitution in 1919.

It could not be concealed, however, that the German monarchs, measured against Bodin's concept of sovereignty, were no longer sovereign, especially as they could not revoke or unilaterally amend the constitutions they had voluntarily enacted. But no one else was sovereign either—certainly not the people. Advocates of liberal constitutional doctrine thus found themselves willing to relativize sovereignty. Johann Caspar Bluntschli, like Constant, explained that "absolutism is not a necessary characteristic of sovereignty; rather, only a constitutionally ordered, limited sovereignty reflects the modern idea of the state; the perfection of the state thus leads from absolute to relative sovereignty."[36]

With the failed Revolution of 1848, liberal constitutional theory, for which Bluntschli was a spokesperson, lost its influence. As in postrevolutionary France, the memory of the excesses of the revolution had a lasting effect and made sovereignty in the absolute sense once again plausible in Germany. However, the difficulties of locating it continued; for although the revolution had failed to achieve its goal of a united and democratic Germany, constitutionalism had asserted itself almost completely, even in Prussia and, with some delay, in the leading restoration power, Austria. Only the two Mecklenburg states remained without a constitution.

The essential catchword that now came to dominate had been provided in the first half of the century by Eduard Albrecht, in a famous review of a traditionally oriented constitutional law treatise by Romeo Maurenbrecher.[37] Albrecht concluded from the constitutional limitations on the monarch that he no longer possessed sovereignty. But it had not vanished; the bearer of sovereignty was instead the state. The monarch, much like the government he installed and the chambers that were partly elected and partly formed from the privileged estates, was merely an organ of this state, though one with a special status under the constitution.

The significance of Albrecht's review was not merely the fact that he understood the consequences of Germany's unique dualist constitutional structure earlier than anyone else.[38] He also indicated a way to defuse one of the period's greatest sources of conflict: by discerning behind the dualism of prince and popular assembly a point of convergence in the form of the state, designated as a legal person. As Helmut Quaritsch correctly emphasized, if one followed Albrecht, "the opposition of king and parliament was no longer identical with the opposition of monarchical and popular sovereignty, absolutism and democracy. Legally speaking, they were organs of a legal person and would no longer argue about such things as divine right of kings and the people's right to self-government, but at most about constitutional powers."[39]

Albrecht thus went beyond G. W. F. Hegel, who had, sixteen years earlier, ascribed sovereignty to the state. He had done this, however, not in order to suggest a third possibility in the fundamental conflict between two claims of sovereignty, monarchical and popular, but to take sides in that dispute, strengthening monarchical claims while contesting the justification for popular sovereignty, which he called one of the "confused ideas" based on the "wild idea of the people." Hegel's concept of state sovereignty did not overcome but rather idealized monarchical sovereignty. The abstract person of the state was, only "real" to him in the form of a natural person, namely the monarch, while the people without a monarch were merely a "formless mass" incapable of forming a state.[40]

In the last third of the nineteenth century, Albrecht's widely accepted views joined with the interpretation of the state as a legal person, without which his views could not have been explained.[41] Constitutional theory thus avoided the difficulty of having to divide or relativize sovereignty. Sovereignty had a single subject, and that subject held it without reservation. Constitutional obligation, as a self-limitation on sovereignty, did not affect the state. It limited not the state, but only its organs. The problem was that the state, as a legal person, could only act through its organs, which had no claim to sovereignty themselves, but only powers.

Following the establishment of the Reich in 1871, some constitutional scholars used this fact to give state sovereignty a pro-monarchical twist. To do so, they introduced an as-yet-unused additional distinction: between the subject and the bearer of sovereignty. The subject was the state, the bearer the monarch. The idea was Hegelian: the monarch could be called sovereign because he "manifests the power due to the state as an imagined person."[42] However, in the constitutional state, he only manifested this power to the extent it was his due and not that of another organ. Jellinek ultimately dispatched this theory by pointing out this contradiction.[43] In the end, the German way of escaping state sovereignty thus had an effect similar to the shift of sovereignty to the people or the nation: within the state, it was absent.

While sovereignty in America and France remained present in the form of the constituent power of the people or nation, this possibility was lacking in Germany. Because the monarch had lost constituent power with the act of imposing the constitution, and this power was not subsequently ascribed to the people, one could only seek it, borrowing from the English "King in Parliament," in the popular assembly and the monarch jointly. Indeed, it was these two organs of the state, and no longer the monarchs alone, that established the constitutions of the North German Confederation and the German Reich by way of treaties.

Because of the absence of sovereignty in the constitutional state and the legal obligation of its organs, H. Krabbe was the first to think of completely separating sovereignty from the state and ascribing it to the legal order.[44] This idea was later radicalized by Hans Kelsen in his assumption that state and law were identical.[45] The state could only be called sovereign to the extent that the legal order of the state was the supreme order. The state is sovereign "as a legal system." Here sovereignty clearly reaches its highest degree of abstraction, no longer reflecting any bearer capable of acting that could exercise the decision-making powers always ascribed to it.

4. SOVEREIGNTY IN THE FEDERAL STATE

In the constitutional state, sovereignty could only remain compatible with separation of powers if it was ascribed to the abstract entity of the state or the fictive entity of the people. In the federal state, things are even more complicated. Here we do not have a single state on one territory, with comprehensive powers that are merely distributed among a number of organs at the level of execution. Instead, several states exist on one and the same territory, each with its own substantively-limited state powers, so that neither the central state nor the component states can claim to possess complete sovereignty. Thus the question of divisibility comes to the fore in the discussion.

There was, however, a credible witness to the possibility of divided sovereignty. Alexis de Tocqueville had emphasized, in his discussion of the United States, that sovereignty there was divided between the central state and the component states. There were "two governments between which sovereignty was going to be apportioned."[46] When we recall the major role played by the idea of indivisibility of sovereignty in the dispute between the colonies and the motherland, and later in the constitutional debates in Philadelphia, Tocqueville's findings sound surprising. On the other hand, Hamilton had promoted adoption of the Constitution by pointing out that it left "certain important portions of sovereign power" to the states.[47]

Still, the sovereignty issue in the United States was hardly resolved with the adoption of the Constitution. The defeated antifederalists insisted on their standpoint that sovereignty remained with the individual states, and therefore interpreted the federal Constitution as a compact among sovereign states, not a decision by the American people.[48] The simmering conflict ignited when the parliament of South Carolina found an 1828 federal law raising import tariffs to be unconstitutional and claimed the right to annul it in South Carolina.

The dispute between "nullifiers" and "unionists" gave rise to two famous debates in the United States Senate on the question of who was empowered to decide the constitutionality of federal laws—the United States (that is, the Supreme Court) or the individual state parliaments. In this debate, Robert Hayne, senator from South Carolina, based his argument on the sovereignty of the individual states. He concluded that, in a conflict regarding the allocation of powers between the states and the United States, the latter did not have the last word, nor did the Supreme Court, because this would equal unlimited rule by the United States in a way that was alien to America. That right to nullify was instead accorded to the individual states.[49]

In his response, Daniel Webster, senator from Massachusetts, did not deny that the individual states were sovereign, but argued that this was the case only "so far as their sovereignty is not affected by this supreme law" (the American Constitution).[50] Thus while he did not mention the phrase, divided sovereignty became conceivable. Webster said nothing more about this, since for him the primary question was who had the last word in such a conflict. In his view, only the federal constitution could provide the answer, and for that answer, in turn, the constitution's source was crucial. "Is it the creature of State legislatures, or the creature of the people?" Webster answered, "It is the people's Constitution." Whatever form state sovereignty took, it was "not sovereign over the people."

In the South Carolina state elections of 1832, the nullification debate was the dominant theme. When the Nullifier Party won the election, Hayne became the state governor. John Calhoun, who had been U.S. vice president after 1825, took Hayne's seat in the U.S. Senate in order to effectively represent South Carolina's interests. The newly elected South Carolina State House immediately scheduled elections to a Popular Congress, which—in purposeful reflection of the wording of the preamble to the U.S. Constitution—declared, "We, the People of the State of South-Carolina, in Convention assembled, do declare and ordain" that the federal laws "are unauthorized by the Constitution of the United States, and violate the true meaning and intent thereof, and are null, void, and no law, nor binding upon this State."[51]

President Andrew Jackson answered by threatening to send troops to South Carolina. A draft law, the so-called Force Bill, was debated in Congress. During the debate, Calhoun defended the lawfulness of nullification.[52] In his view, the right arose from the continued sovereignty of the individual states, for which the United States was merely an "agent." The United States owed its existence not to the American people, but to the individual states. The constitution they had called into being was by its nature a treaty among sovereign states. By signing the treaty, they had neither given up their sovereignty nor shared it with the United States. Shared sovereignty was conceptually impossible. "Sovereignty is an entire thing:—to divide is,—to destroy it."[53]

Calhoun emphasized the difference between "sovereignty" and "sovereign powers." Only the "sovereign powers" were divided between the United States and the individual states, while sovereignty itself remained with the individual states. Only they could decide upon the "reserved powers." An act of the United States that affected these was unconstitutional and void. In Calhoun's view, the continued sovereignty of the individual states meant that they had decision-making authority in conflicts over distribution of powers—not the Supreme Court, which was part of the "general government" and thus could only judge "delegated powers," not "reserved powers." "The reservation of powers to the States is . . . as full against the judicial as it is against the executive and the legislative departments of the Government."[54]

Webster answered Calhoun without dwelling on the possibility of shared sovereignty.[55] Instead, he denied that the dispute really concerned the problem of sovereignty. "It is not a contest between two sovereigns for the same power." The dispute played out below the level of sovereignty. While he had spoken in his 1830 speech of divided sovereignty, now he spoke of divided powers. "It is the case of a division of powers between two governments, made by the people." Neither of these two governments was sovereign. It was a European idea that the government was entitled to sovereignty. "But with us, all power is with the people. They alone are sovereign."

The crucial issue then became the source and legal nature of the federal constitution: Was it a treaty among sovereign states, "a constitutional compact," as Calhoun had expressed it, or a constitution enacted by the people? The two possibilities were mutually exclusive, "a constitution of government and a compact between sovereign powers being things essentially unlike in their very natures, and incapable of ever being the same." The division of powers among the individual states and the United States had been established in the Constitution by the American people. That alone regulated who could resolve conflicts regarding distribution of powers. "The Supreme Court of the United States is the final interpreter." States that claimed this right for themselves were engaging in a revolution.

In his response, Calhoun insisted that the U.S. Constitution was indeed a treaty.[56] To Webster's objection that it might have come about as a treaty, but was by its legal nature a constitution, he responded that a treaty was a treaty. Only the individual states could have been parties to the treaty—not the United States, which had emerged only on the basis of the treaty, and not the American people, since it was the people of the individual states who had ratified the treaty. This also distinguished it from the earlier confederation. "The confederation was the act of the

State governments, and formed a union of governments. The present constitution is the act of the States themselves, or, which is the same thing, of the people of the several States, and forms a union of them as sovereign communities."[57]

The conflict between the United States and South Carolina was settled, in the end, through a change in customs laws. But this did not settle the controversy over who was sovereign in the federal state. That question would ultimately be decided only by the American Civil War. Yet the idea of divisible sovereignty always resonated as a third possibility. Even the Supreme Court proceeded from the notion of divided sovereignty in an early decision on the distribution of powers between the U.S. and the individual states and continues to do so today.[58] Tocqueville's portrayal thus does not seem completely wrong. It helped the Europeans to resolve their own sovereignty conflicts—first Switzerland, and then, at least for a time, Germany.

In the case of Switzerland, the problem emerged—as it would later in Germany—in connection with the issue of national unity.[59] During the Napoleonic era, Switzerland had briefly been a unified state, under the name Helvetic Republic. It became a confederation again in 1815, after Napoleon's fall from power. As had happened sixty years earlier in America, however, the weaknesses of the confederation were increasingly felt to be a flaw. After the Sonderbund War between the Protestant and Catholic cantons, a change seemed unavoidable. The Tagsatzung, the cantons' joint organ at the confederacy level, therefore appointed a commission to draft proposals to reform the articles of confederation.

As in America, however, this commission soon came to the conclusion that a reform of the confederation was not enough. Switzerland had to be transformed into a federal state, and its articles of confederation into a constitution. A majority would be enough to bring the constitution into force. This process could not be derived from the articles of confederation of 1815. Thus the step was no less revolutionary than the proceedings at the Philadelphia Convention. Here, too, the question of sovereignty necessarily took a prominent role. On the one hand, it was clear that no state could be established if the federation were not sovereign. On the other, it was certain that there was no majority for eliminating cantonal sovereignty.

In Switzerland, however, unlike in America, the solution was sought not in popular sovereignty overarching a federation and member states, although it was recognized that the authority of the federation came from the Swiss people. The Swiss—less well informed theoretically, but also less handicapped than the Americans by the prior debates with England—agreed to the formula, which has held to this day, that the cantons were sovereign to the extent their sovereignty was not limited by the federal constitution. This meant nothing less than divided sovereignty. They felt vindicated in their assumption that this was possible by the United States, as Tocqueville had reported the solution there.

In Germany, too, the sovereignty question arose in connection with the formation of the Reich. In the German Confederation it had seemed unproblematic because the Confederation, like the American Confederation of 1787, had been formed as a treaty-based union of states, which possessed no sovereignty of its own and thus did not call into question the sovereignty of the member states. Still, the German Confederation in fact had more powers than the American Confederation, particularly in resisting democratic aspirations among its member states. The decisions of its organ, the Federal Assembly, were binding on the member states, and the Confederation could even use force against reluctant members.

This, too, would have been compatible with sovereignty, as a commitment by the member states themselves, if the Federal Assembly had been required to make decisions unanimously. But unanimity was only required on important matters, whereas on less important ones a majority sufficed. It was thus possible for a member state to be bound by a decision to which it had not agreed. As long as that was possible, it was subject to a higher power. Some constitutional scholars thus saw an irregularity in the confederation that did not fit the dualism of confederation and federated state. Others later argued that the sovereignty of the member states had not first been breached with the formation of the German Reich, but earlier in the German Confederation.

Yet any attempt in Germany to follow the example of the United States or Switzerland had to raise the question of sovereignty. In the Revolution of 1848 it was answered in favor of the Reich. The National Assembly, like the Philadelphia Convention, considered its task from the outset to be not reform of the confederation but adoption of a national constitution. Unlike the American Convention, however, it had a mandate from the people. As in the United States, the basis for the constitution's legitimacy was supposed to be popular sovereignty. Here the people meant not the sum of the people of the individual states, but the German people in its entirety. In his opening address, the president of the assembly, Heinrich von Gagern, left no doubt of this: "We shall create a constitution for Germany, for the entire Reich. The calling and mandate for this creation lies in the sovereignty of the nation."[60]

With the failure of the revolution and the subsequent Prussian plan for a union, the confederation was revived, and with it the recognition of the sovereignty of the individual state princes. Certainly this did not extinguish hopes for a German nation-state. But the failure of the attempt to create national unity from below fostered the belief that its success was only possible in association with the princes, not against them. Those who continued to pursue the idea of national unity thus had to prove the compatibility of a federal state and monarchical sovereignty. Historian Georg Waitz of Göttingen undertook to demonstrate this possibility in a study, published in 1853, on "The Nature of the Federal State."[61]

Waitz addressed Joseph Maria Radowitz's thesis that the Revolution of 1848 was bound to fail because it was impossible to form a federal state out of monarchies. In this view, an essential feature of a kingdom was monarchical sovereignty, which could not be maintained in a federal state that claimed sovereignty for itself.[62] If this were accurate, a nation-state could only emerge in Germany after the individual states were transformed into republics or incorporated into a united state—the one as unlikely as the other and, therefore, for supporters of national unity, an irritating idea.

Waitz, a former deputy of the Frankfurt Assembly and a member of its constitutional committee, now countered "that the nature of the federal state is in itself not at all inconsistent with the concept of the kingdom." The kingdom, in its full sense, required the monarch to possess an independent right to rule, not merely one transferred to it, "whether from a higher ruler or from the people." What the concept of the kingdom did not require was "the uniting of all state power and activity in one person." Waitz did not doubt that, in a federal state, both the central state and the member states possessed the character of states. Because the state was not conceivable without sovereignty, however, the only conclusion possible was that both the central state and the member states were sovereign.

But if the central state could attain sovereignty without the founding states losing theirs, their existence as states was no longer at stake; the only issue was the appropriate division of powers between the central state and the member states. Waitz thus did not hesitate to abandon the idea of the unity of sovereignty. Sovereignty still meant being the supreme power. But it was enough that every state belonging to the federal state was supreme "in its sphere" and could therefore exercise its powers independently of other states. He, too, referred to the United States, as he perceived it through Tocqueville's lens.

Waitz's "as well as" now stood alongside the "either ... or" of the stark contraposition of nonsovereign confederation and solely sovereign federal state. This appealed to the political hopes of the German bourgeoisie: the nation-state did not come at an unaffordable price. The princes could retain what they most valued, which ensured Waitz's doctrine broad acceptance His thesis dominated scholarship from the 1850s on; this was confirmed by Heinrich von Treitschke, the leading historian of the epoch, who concurred with Waitz's views in his 1864 study *Federal State and Unitary State* and gave him credit for explaining Hamilton's groundbreaking ideas about the federal state "systematically and with the great seriousness of German scholarship... "The old struggle among the schools over the concept of confederation and federal state has been concluded with this masterly study by Waitz."[63]

The true challenge, however, came with the formation of the North German Confederation and soon after the German Reich in 1871. The negotiations on its founding were already difficult due to the sovereignty issue. Otto von Bismarck therefore preferred to conceal the sovereignty problem. According to his directive on the Reich Constitution, the Reich should be a federal state in essence, but should seem to be a confederation in form. This contradiction was essentially bridged by not mentioning the sovereignty issue in the text of the Reich Constitution. Politically, this ambiguity was a condition for adoption of the Constitution. But scholars could not leave the question open if they were to systematically comprehend the legal nature of the Reich and draw doctrinal conclusions from it.

The question left unanswered politically thus quickly became the central legal issue. No subject in constitutional law or the theory of the state was dealt with as intensively as sovereignty in the federal state. Every renowned public law scholar and numerous other writers took part in the discussion. It was begun spectacularly by a young Bavarian jurist, Max Seydel, in his first book, *The Concept of the Federal State,* in 1872. In it he addressed Waitz's theory of dual sovereignty, calling it theoretically untenable because it contradicted the nature of the state. To prove this, he relied upon arguments by Calhoun, whose views he laid out in detail.[64]

In contrast to the approach taken until then, Seydel sought to understand the nature of the federal state not through the concept of sovereignty but through the concept of the state. He viewed the state as the supreme form of human community—the "union of the people of a country under one supreme will." There was no higher "union" than the state, no equal one next to it. "Therefore, a state beside a state on the same territory is impossible, because a dual perfect union is a contradictio in adiecto." This unity could only be governed by a unified supreme will. "Two supreme wills cancel each other out." In this argument the will appeared in the form of state power. It was the supreme power and tolerated no other power above or next to itself. Since Bodin, Seydel explained, the expression *sovereign* had described this characteristic of state power.

Seydel approached the concept of the federal state from this starting point, disputing Waitz's doctrine of dual sovereignty and taking Calhoun as a basis. Like the latter, he believed divided sovereignty to be logically impossible. Consequently, in a federal state, the central state and the member states could not be sovereign simultaneously. This was not all, however. Because the state was defined by sovereignty, the central state and the member states could not be states simultaneously. If this was so, however, the possibility of a federal state disappeared entirely. And Seydel did indeed draw this conclusion: "All state entities that one identifies with the name federal state must be either simple states or federations of states." There was no third way between a confederation and a unitary state.

Under these circumstances, Seydel could not then avoid the question of what earned the name *state* in the new Reich—the central state or the member states. He sought the answer—once again following Calhoun—in the origins of federal states. They came about through treaties among existing unitary states. As a consequence, their character as states depended on whether the states concluding the treaties intended to give up their sovereignty and transfer it to the newly created polity. Because there could be no nonsovereign state, the question was, more precisely, whether they gave up their existence as states upon concluding the treaty. To Seydel, no such intention was discernible at the formation of the Reich. Consequently, the Reich had not attained sovereignty, and, also consequently, it had not become a state. It had remained a federation under a new name.

Seydel's thesis triggered a very prolific debate on the concept of the federal state.[65] Waitz's dualist theory, designed to demonstrate the possibility of national unity under postrevolutionary conditions, did not survive the creation of the nation-state. On this point, Seydel won hands down. "Sovereignty is a quality with an absolute character that allows of no increase or reduction. ... There is no half, divided, reduced, dependent, relative sovereignty but only sovereignty or non-sovereignty," argued Paul Laband in his representative treatise.[66] Treitschke, who had so highly praised Waitz in 1864, distanced himself from him ten years later.[67] Only a few authors of the older generation clung to the idea of the divisibility of sovereignty.

In contrast, Seydel failed to prevail with his view that a federal state was logically impossible and that there could only be unitary states or confederations. On this point, he found only a single supporter, Philipp Zorn.[68] But Zorn drew the opposite conclusion from Seydel's premises: The Reich was a unitary state; its members were not states, but were only called so. The majority of authors, however, did not conclude, from the premise of the indivisibility of sovereignty, that no federal state was possible. They believed it was possible to create an overall union out of individual units in which both had the quality of states.

However, a price had to be paid for this assumption elsewhere. It could only be maintained if the state and sovereignty no longer necessarily went hand in hand, but were divisible. A political unit could have the quality of a state without being sovereign. This was in fact the conclusion drawn by the majority of authors. Laband explained this innovation by pointing out that the sovereignty theory developed through consideration of unitary states; for these, it might seem as though state and sovereignty were conditional upon one another. But the emergence of composite states required a refinement of the theory.[69]

This refinement was then developed by Georg Jellinek. Jellinek proclaimed it a fundamental error in sovereignty theory that state power had been identified with sovereignty.[70] Sovereignty should, more correctly, be seen not as the essence of state power but merely as one characteristic, the absence of which did not affect the existence of state power. The only essential aspect of the state was state power, not sovereignty. Seydel protested that one could call nonsovereign states "states, only in the same sense that one calls a eunuch a man."[71] But his objection was in vain; the doctrine of the separability of state and sovereignty prevailed.

Its supporters had, of course, to explain what in these circumstances turned a political community into a state and how it differed from a province, municipality, etc.; and also how state power would have to be constituted to be considered sovereign. The criteria were quite varied. In regard to statehood, most agreed with Laband that specific powers were sufficient; Jellinek's addendum, however, that these powers could not be monitored by someone else was largely rejected.[72] The possibility of monitoring whether a member state had acted within the scope of its powers did not rob it of its sovereignty.

In regard to sovereignty, there was no change in the starting point that it was the main, supreme, independent state power. As such, it could not be increased or decreased. It was a superlative. If that were the extent of it, however, sovereignty would be a purely negative concept, defined only by the absence of a superior power. However, Jellinek placed particular weight on the idea that supreme power was not to be confused with unlimited power.[73] The sovereign state was unlimited only in regard to external limitations, because otherwise it would have a higher power above it. But internal limitations, as a form of self-limitation, did not contradict sovereignty.

Jellinek saw self-limitation not only as a possibility, but even as a necessity, because a state without law was unimaginable. A lawless state would descend into anarchy. It could not desire its own negation. Where there is a state, there is also law, and the state is therefore bound by law. By virtue of its sovereignty, the state may abolish or change any concrete self-imposed limitations in regard to existing law. But it is not above the law to such an extent that it can completely avoid being bound by law. Thus Jellinek defined sovereignty as the "characteristic of state power, by virtue of which it has the exclusive ability of legal self-determination and self-limitation."[74]

For the federal state, this means that the division of powers between the central state and the member states that characterizes it does not affect sovereignty as long as it is a self-limitation. What is crucial for sovereignty in a federal state is not the extent of state power, but only who determines its distribution. One who establishes one's own powers oneself, and therefore determines the powers of the other side, is sovereign. In other words, what is crucial for sovereignty in a federal state is *Kompetenz-Kompetenz* (the power to distribute powers). In *Kompetenz-Kompetenz*, sovereignty retreats.[75] This became the general belief, and thus the sovereignty of the Reich was established.

Albert Hänel, one of the few critics of Laband, agreed with this view.[76] However, he also took a position outside the strict dualism of central state and member states that the other authors advocated. Hänel considered this dualism to be a mechanistic dispersal of the state's task that failed to do justice to the reality of the federal state, which consisted in the "organic affiliation and systematic cooperation of the two." Neither side alone, nor both with their special positions, constituted the state, in his view. "Not the individual state, nor the central state, are states per se; they are only polities organized and acting as states do. A state per se is only the federal state, as the totality of both."

Thus one can see Hänel as the precursor of the theory of the "three-branch federal state." This idea can be attributed to Kelsen, who saw both the central state and the member states as partial systems, distinguished only by their different powers; above them existed the common state, which was the actual federal state and an expression of the unity of the whole.[77] Its only function was to grant the partial systems their powers; in other words, it determined the common constitution, upon which both the constitution of the central state and the constitutions of the member states were based. Thus it had *Kompetenz-Kompetenz* and therefore sovereignty in the traditional sense.

However, Kelsen had to deal with the objection,[78] already raised against Hänel by Laband, that this superordinate state was not visible in either a separate constitution or separate organs. Only the central state's constitution and its organs were above the member states. Nevertheless, Kelsen viewed the common constitution as positive law, not merely a logical legal condition.[79] But because there is no third constitutional text, the common constitution can only be contained within the central state's constitution. Therefore, the body permitted to amend this constitution acts in different capacities depending on whether the norms being changed can be attributed to the common constitution or the central state's constitution. The fact that it does not appear this way is simply the result of "a narrowing of perspective."[80]

Kelsen's great opponent, Carl Schmitt, found the coexistence of several independent political units within a common legal framework (in his terminology a *Bund*) troubling and a contradiction in terms.[81]

Nevertheless, he asserted that there is sovereignty in the federation and that sovereignty is undivided. But the *Bund* can persist only if the question of who is sovereign is left open. As soon as the question is posed, the *Bund* collapses. Either the several subunits lose their independence or the higher unit disappears. What allows the *Bund* to leave the sovereignty question open is the homogeneity of the parts, which Schmitt regards as a precondition of a *Bund*. Homogeneity makes it possible for no part to play the sovereign vis-à-vis the others.

Shortly after Schmitt had developed these ideas, Hitler came to power and abolished the federal system in Germany. It was reestablished after World War II by the Allies, but again abolished in East Germany. In West German federalism, the sovereignty question played no role. In its external relations, the Federal Republic was not completely sovereign before unification. Internally, the federal system gave rise to many constitutional questions, but there was no theoretical or political discourse regarding who was sovereign in the Federal Republic. It was taken for granted that sovereignty belonged to the Federal Republic. Neither did the Federal Constitutional Court discuss federalism problems in terms of sovereignty. The question reappeared only in connection with the European Union, when all the arguments from the nineteenth century surfaced once again.[82]

5. LATENT SOVEREIGNTY

With the American and French revolutions, the project of modern constitutionalism was definitively established. The modern constitution was not one of those innovations that emerge in rudimentary form and mature only in the course of time. With these prototypes, the *achievement* of constitutionalism emerged fully formed and set the standard against which all later constitutions would be measured. In content, constitutions may vary greatly. But if they lack the structural elements that are constitutive for constitutions, while they may still fulfill many of the functions of a constitution and even be called "constitutions," they are not constitutions in the fullest sense of the achievement that emerged from the revolutions.[83]

The question is how the emergence of the constitutional state affected sovereignty. On the one hand, the constitutional state did not abandon sovereignty—certainly not external sovereignty, since this is measured by international law and not domestic constitutional law; but also not internal sovereignty. On the other hand, it is one of the characteristics of a constitutional state that it recognizes no supreme power in the state. There are only various state powers that specialize in particular functions granted them by the constitution. Even the legislative power is subject to law in a constitutional state—that is, to higher constitutional law.

The meaning of the modern constitution is, in fact, the comprehensive regulation of public authority. Through the constitution, the establishment and exercise of state authority are subject to thorough regulation, derived from a few basic principles. "Comprehensive" and "thorough," however, should not be confused with total regulation. The constitution regulates politics, but does not make it unnecessary. Total regulation would mean reducing politics to the implementation of the constitution, thus robbing politics of its political content. The constitutional claim to regulate is comprehensive in the sense that neither extraconstitutional bearers of governmental powers, nor extraconstitutional ways and means of exercising public power, are permitted.

Because the situation was different before constitutionalization, sovereignty could not remain untouched by the transformation of the monarchical state into a constitutional state. The sovereignty of the constitutional state differs from that of previous political entities. Since none of the powers constituted by the constitution can claim to be sovereign, the constitution and sovereignty can only be reconciled by locating sovereignty's bearers outside the constituted powers. In the constitutions that emerged from the American and French revolutions, no one but the people could take on this function. But even predemocratic constitutionalism, such as Germany's in the nineteenth century, had to pay tribute to this result of the constitution, substituting the state for the people.

Yet not only historical but also systemic reasons supported a separation of sovereignty from state powers. The regulation of public authority intended by the constitution required that none of the powers be above the law. Since law was no longer found, however, but had to be made, the portion of law that constituted and regulated state power had to be attributed to a different source. Only the people were available, since any other source of legitimacy—be it transcendental or elitist—would have endangered the function of the constitution. Sovereignty in the fully formed constitutional state is popular sovereignty.

This has a range of consequences for the concept of sovereignty. The basic characteristic that has been maintained from the beginning—that sovereignty means supreme power—is unaffected. Only someone who, in regard to his powers, is subject to and legally dependent on no one can be called sovereign. The same is true of the elements that distinguish the modern concept of sovereignty from its medieval counterpart. Supreme power means more than the ability to make irreversible decisions. Whether the indivisibility of sovereignty could be maintained, however, remained unclear once it was acknowledged that, in addition to unitary states, the possibility of states comprised of states existed.

The remaining elements of Bodin's concept of sovereignty, in contrast, do not comport with the constitutional state. They must be abandoned or adapted. This is especially true of the holder of sovereignty. In the Middle Ages, sovereignty was always connected with a person, and Bodin, too, could only imagine the sovereign as an individual or group of people. The attempt by monarchical constitutionalists to ascribe sovereignty—as in the French Charter of 1814—to a person, the monarch, was unsuccessful because it was not compatible with the characteristic of supreme and independent power. The constitutional monarch clearly could not make decisions alone in every area.

But even if sovereignty were ascribed to the people or the nation, it seems difficult to speak of personal possession of sovereignty. The concept of the nation already suggests a "supra-individual" unity that is more than the sum of the people currently living in a territory. But the people, as the sum of individuals, are also difficult to imagine as a personal holder of sovereignty, at least if one considers the ability to make decisions to be part of sovereignty. If we limit the people to the active citizens, they are not the entire people. If we include all citizens, they lack the ability to act.

The deeper reason for the impossibility of a personal holder of sovereignty in the constitutional state, however, lies in the fact that in such a state the holding and exercising of state power must be separate. It is the very meaning of constitutionalism that those who have public authority over others are not granted sovereignty. They are merely organs of a political entity and may only use the powers granted them and the instruments of power entrusted to them within the limits drawn by the constitution and under the conditions set by it. It follows from this that there is no sovereignty in a constitutional state, but only powers. Sovereignty withdraws into the constituent power and expresses itself only in the act of constitution making. As long as the constitution is in force, it remains latent.[84]

Confirmation of this can be found in the minor importance of the concept of sovereignty to the interpretation and application of constitutions. It was instead membership in the European Union that raised the question of sovereignty in constitutional jurisprudence. The question was the degree to which states could transfer certain powers to international organizations without losing their sovereignty. The French constitution devotes its first section to sovereignty, though without determining the content of the term. It does not, like the constitution of 1791, name the properties of sovereignty ("one, indivisible, imprescriptible and unalienable," Title III, article 1). The Constitutional Council at first distinguished between the impermissible "transfer" of sovereignty and its permissible "limitation." Today it speaks of a "transfer of competences," while the "essential conditions of the exercise of national sovereignty" must be ensured.[85]

In Germany, where "sovereignty" does not appear in the Basic Law, the Federal Constitutional Court assumed, in its Maastricht judgment, that the Federal Republic remains sovereign even as a member state of the European Union; however, to the extent that powers have been transferred, it exercises its sovereignty together with other member states.[86] In its Lisbon judgment, the court, like the French Constitutional Council, emphasized the difference between sovereignty, which inheres in the member states, and sovereign or governmental powers, which may be transferred, albeit only to a certain extent. The court also expanded on its conclusion that Germany continued to be sovereign, stating that the Basic Law not only presumes the Federal Republic to be a sovereign state but in fact guarantees it. It is empowered to transfer powers to the European Union only on condition that German sovereignty is preserved. The Basic Law does not allow the German people's right of self-determination, in the form of sovereignty under international law, to be surrendered.[87]

For the United States, too, in whose emergence the sovereignty issue was of crucial importance, it was international developments, particularly the tendency toward the creation of institutions that can override national sovereignty, that revived sovereignty as a constitutional problem apart from federalism issues. Sovereignty under international law has been deployed as a defense of the American Constitution, with its grounding in popular sovereignty. Sovereignty functions to protect democracy against an international legal order that has no claim to democratic legitimacy.[88]

The observation that sovereignty is latent in the constitutional state does not apply only to representative democracy, which grants the people decision-making powers through elections alone. Where the people possess additional decision-making powers, such as referenda, they exercise them as powers created and regulated by the constitution. They act as a constituted power. This is sometimes obscured terminologically, as in article 3 of the French constitution, which states that the people exercise national sovereignty through their representatives and even through referenda. Here, too, sovereignty is not reintroduced into the constitutional state. The people do not express themselves as sovereign in a referendum.

One can even ask whether amending the constitution can be viewed as an act of sovereignty. This is certainly not the case if the constitution grants state bodies the power to amend the text, and even less so if it limits them to amendments that conform to the system, as in article 89 of the French constitution and article 79 (3) of the Basic Law. In this case the difference between *pouvoir constituant* and *pouvoir constitué* is reflected in the amendment process. The greater significance of the amendment power is expressed in the requirement of a qualified majority. But only the creation of a new constitution is an act in which popular sovereignty is expressed.[89]

However, we know that, even in the act of creating a new constitution, for example following a revolutionary break with the old order, social groups appear on the scene claiming to act in the name of the people, and, if successful, bring the people into play, either in electing deputies to draft a new constitution or in adopting such a draft. But the validity of a new constitution does not depend on direct popular participation. Even its acceptance and legitimacy do not necessarily depend upon it. In Germany no constitution has enjoyed greater legitimacy than the Basic Law, which was never directly sanctioned by the people, whereas the Weimar Constitution, drafted by a National Assembly elected solely for this purpose, quickly lost its legitimacy.[90]

This ultimately demonstrates that the constitutional state has made the sovereign invisible. Popular sovereignty is not a reality, but an ascription. The sovereign remains only an abstract subject for the ascription of acts of public authority. This does not mean that recognizing the people as a subject for ascription has no practical significance. Popular sovereignty may be a fiction,[91] but the fact that the people are recognized as the source of public authority, to whom the exercise of power must be accountable, yields real consequences that account for differences between political regimes.[92] This is one reason that the constitution is considered an achievement.

It was Carl Schmitt who formulated the protest against displacing sovereignty with constitutionalism. However, he too was unable to return sovereignty to its prior status without depriving the constitutional state of its meaning. He could, however, weaken the constitutional state. He did this by restricting the applicability of constitutional law to normal circumstances. In his view, sovereignty could only remain latent under such circumstances. In times of emergency, however, constitutional law had to be abandoned, and unlimited state power prevailed. In emergencies, sovereignty was revived. "Sovereign is he who decides on the exception."[93]

A state of emergency, in Schmitt's view, was by definition impervious to legal regulation. He was not speaking of predictable disturbances of limited scope, which were provided for by a constitution's emergency provisions. But for emergencies that threatened the very existence of the nation, the constitution could at best prescribe who might act. Because the existence of a true state of emergency cannot be defined in advance, and the means of overcoming it cannot be statutorily prescribed, Schmitt refused to treat emergency powers as legal competences. Whoever is empowered to act is sovereign, and his "decisions are free of any normative bonds and are absolute in the actual sense."[94]

Schmitt's idea of sovereignty was thus the flip side of the sovereignty realized through the constitution-making power. It was a constitution-unmaking power.[95] In contrast to the constituent power, however, he did not ascribe this power to the people, who cannot act in times of emergency, but to a ruler who legitimizes himself through his successful actions in time of emergency. Schmitt did not indicate what would follow once the state of emergency was overcome. During the Weimar Constitution's existential crisis in 1932, however, he did not support the idea that only a desire to rescue the constitution could justify its temporary suspension. Schmitt's doctrine of sovereignty led away from the constitutional state.[96]

External Sovereignty

I. SOVEREIGNTY IN THE WESTPHALIAN ERA

The epochal transformation wrought by Bodin upon the concept of sovereignty in the sixteenth century was motivated by domestic politics. Concentrating the scattered powers of governance into a comprehensive public power situated in a single hand and extending them to lawmaking were conditions for overcoming civil war and pacifying society. But this had consequences for international politics. Unified territories formed as a result of this concept; they were now the locus of public power now referred to them. It was no longer defined personally, but territorially. People were subject to rulers based on their territorial connections.

The crucial phenomenon in understanding modern sovereignty, in contrast to its medieval counterpart, is the territorialization of political rule by means of state formation.[1] State rule is territorially limited rule.

This creates a distinction between the internal and the external and, in relation to people, between nationals and foreigners;[2] the formation of national identities can be linked to these distinctions. Sovereignty is then manifested not only in control over the inhabitants of a territory but also in the ability to control ones' own borders. This does not mean borders are impermeable, but that movement across them can be monitored.

The distinction between internal and external sovereignty necessarily accompanied the territorialization of political rule.[3] A ruler was sovereign only in his territory. Outside of it, there were other sovereigns who made the same claim for their own territories. This allowed a distinction to be made between internal and external aspects of sovereignty; yet only if both existed could a ruler be considered sovereign. It was not enough that there was no higher ruler internally. One had also to be free from any external control. The kinds of political pressures that can result from various power relationships were not enough, however, to form the basis for such subjection. For sovereignty as a legal status, all that mattered was freedom from subjugation to other rulers.

All sovereigns were equal in their legal independence, regardless of differences in actual power. Their legal relationships could therefore be based only on coordination and not on subordination. Thus an external law emerged—international law—that was distinct from constitutional, or internal, law. This, too, was a result of the territorialization of rule. It was territorialization that made legal regulation of external relations possible and necessary. The international law that emerged in the sixteenth century, with the formation of states, was thus different from the Roman *ius gentium*, although the word served as the basis for its translation into various languages.

For the formation of this type of law, it was also significant that the change from a personal to a territorial reference point in political rule made it possible to distinguish between the person of the ruler and the independent, spatially defined political association. This could be raised to a higher level of abstraction and conceived of as a state, even if—as was common in the phase when states were emerging—its sole representative was found in the person of the ruler. In contrast to internal sovereignty, which would remain linked to the person of the ruler for some time, modern international law referred from the start to the relationship among states, which were seen as legal persons in themselves.

International law, specializing in external relations among states, was not concerned with a state's internal order. Human rights, which would later become a major theme in the legitimation of rule and would change internal sovereignty, could not be portrayed in international law. How the state treated its subjects was irrelevant to international law. It could also ignore the questions about the substance and holders of sovereignty that accompanied the development of internal sovereignty—questions that were often highly controversial and led to varying answers depending on circumstances. The concept of sovereignty in international law thus remained more stable than in constitutional law. It did not need to undergo all the changes experienced by internal sovereignty.

The fact that sovereign states were the legal subjects of international law ruled out the existence of a higher body above them that made and implemented law. This would have been tantamount to eliminating state sovereignty. International law thus consisted of customary law, which owed its validity not to acts of legislation but to a shared belief that it was law, and above all to norms agreed upon by treaty that bound only the parties to the treaty. Contractual bonds did not affect sovereignty because they imposed no external obligations on the state; they were self-imposed, corresponding to other sovereign states' self-imposed commitments.

The fact that international law was based on the equal claim to sovereignty of all states required some general legal precepts, the existence and recognition of which were necessary for a legal system that was primarily based on treaties. The validity of these legal precepts did not depend on express agreement. The first of these necessary norms was the principle of *pacta sunt servanda.* Further, a prohibition on intervention in a state's domestic affairs was implicit in the concept of the sovereignty of the legal subjects of international law, because intervention would have abrogated sovereignty. This was the case no matter how internal sovereignty was organized or dealt with.

Classical international law was essentially designed on the basis of internal sovereignty and built a protective barrier around it. At no point did it go beyond the external relations of states; it empowered and obligated only states, but not citizens. It had no influence whatsoever on domestic law. If an international legal obligation was to have domestic applicability, the state had to transform it into domestic law. The state could, in some circumstances, be required to do this. But there was no legal way to enforce a treaty obligation. Nor was there a general rule of primacy that would have resolved such a conflict.

The lack of a supranational authority to enforce law resulted in a situation in which the domestic pacification tool, the monopoly of force, was not available at the level of relations among states. Unlike the members of a federation, the states therefore retained the right to use force to enforce the law. In addition, the lack of a supranational authority prevented an authoritative determination of legal issues. The states therefore also had the power to determine whether they were acting lawfully. The situation thus resembled the state of nature in natural law doctrine, from which the authors had derived the justification for the state.

However, the literature on international law, which rapidly flourished, developed criteria to judge whether wars were just or unjust (*ius ad bellum*), and established rules for the behavior of belligerents in wartime (*ius in bello*). This was made easier by the fact that the universal Christian order that had emerged before the schism could serve as a point of reference.[4] Grotius's 1625 work *De iure belli ac pacis,* which is often considered the beginning of modern international law, also focused "less on international law than on the design of a universal Christian legal order," though without the medieval centerpieces of empire, emperor, and pope.[5]

This international legal order is frequently dated to the Peace of Westphalia in 1648 and described as "Westphalian," because that is where it found its first manifestation in positive law. In the *Instrumentum Pacis Osnabrugensis*, the territorial power of the estates and free cities of the empire was recognized, while sovereignty was attributed to the empire itself. Notwithstanding, the territorial powers in the empire were granted the right to form alliances among themselves and with foreign powers, which had been denied by the Peace of Prague in 1635, provided that they did not use them against the emperor and the empire.

2. DEVELOPMENTS IN THE TWENTIETH CENTURY

This order remained stable for many centuries. This does not mean that it was always adhered to or that it experienced no changes. Martti Koskenniemi has pointed to significant transformations in international legal scholarship, especially since the last third of the nineteenth century.[6] But the system's basis in sovereignty—states as the sole subjects of international law, with the right of internal self-determination, secured by the prohibition on intervention, and therefore with external independence, binding themselves legally only through treaties—was not called into question.

The system had weaknesses, however. On the question whether a state had violated the rights of another state, or whether legal claims were valid, each was its own judge. No guarantee existed that force would be used only to enforce law. There was certainly no international protection if a state deprived its own citizens of their rights. The applicability of international law presupposed a political entity with the attributes of statehood, regardless of its legitimacy. Even genocide domestically did not justify outside intervention. The resolution of international disputes was dependent on treaty agreements between the states affected. No higher dispute-resolution body existed above them.

Yet since World War II this system has been undergoing a fundamental transformation, though it is not entirely without precedent.[7] In the nineteenth century, treaty relations between states had already become far more dense, mainly due to the need for regulation created by scientific and technical progress. At the end of the nineteenth century, efforts were initiated to ensure a permanent peace; they included numerous states and culminated in the Hague Peace Conference, which in 1899 produced the multilateral Convention for the Pacific Settlement of International Disputes, as well as numerous additional treaties, including the Hague Convention Respecting the Laws and Customs of War on Land in 1907.

Following World War I, at the initiative of the United States but without America's involvement, the League of Nations was formed, as well as the Permanent Court of International Justice in The Hague in 1922. The members of the League of Nations agreed to guarantee the territorial integrity and political independence of its member states and, in case of violations, to impose sanctions on the violator state. The league itself, however, could not use coercive force against states. It could make unanimous recommendations for preserving world peace and could take preventive measures, but these did not go beyond reprimands and proposals.

The Permanent Court of International Justice—unlike its predecessor, the Permanent Court of Arbitration in The Hague created in 1899 as the first international judicial body—was not an arbitral panel but a real court. Its judges were chosen by the organized community of nations, not by the parties themselves. However, the court had no general jurisdiction over international legal disputes among member states. Its jurisdiction was established ad hoc, by agreement of the parties to the dispute. The court could hear a case only if a state had previously accepted its jurisdiction.

The changes in the first half of the twentieth century thus did not demolish the foundations of the classical international legal order. They led to a tighter network of treaty-based obligations among states, and a larger number of states were tied into a system of collective alliances. But there was still no possibility of obligating a state to act against its will or forcing it to cease acting. The prohibition on intervention in internal affairs also remained unaffected. The changes left state sovereignty undiminished. The bounds of traditional sovereignty were only crossed in the wake of World War II.

The turning point was the formation of the United Nations in 1945. Though modeled organizationally on the League of Nations, its powers went far beyond those of its predecessor. It is true that, under article 2 of the UN Charter, the UN is also based on the sovereign equality of all its member states. But after the experience of the League of Nations, it was clear from the outset that it could only achieve its main goal—maintaining international peace and security and taking effective collective measures to that end, as article 1 of the charter provides—if state sovereignty were curtailed. Therefore, the members of the UN gave up their right to use force to assert legal rights. Military action is now only permitted for the purpose of self-defense against aggression.

If the matter had ended with this renunciation, however, the limits of traditional international law would not yet have been demolished. This only happened with the UN's empowerment to use force to ensure world peace against those who would disturb it. The UN cannot do this using its own means, as it has neither the personnel nor the substantive resources for military operations. It must depend on military contingents placed at its disposal by the member states. When this happens, however, the troops act not at the behest of their states, but by UN mandate, and answer to an international commander. The affected states cannot invoke their sovereignty in regard to such operations.

The UN's decision-making body for collective measures is the Security Council, in which each of the five permanent members has the veto power under article 27(3) of the charter. During the period of the Cold War, the veto power largely prevented collective action. Since the worldwide political transformation in 1989–90, however, the UN has, in the course of maintaining peace, increasingly displayed supranational powers that reach into states and supplant their own sovereign rights. While we cannot yet speak of the Security Council as a world legislature, under article 25 of the charter, it is permitted to take norm-creating measures that bind states.

In the context of increased protection of human rights, too, the prohibition on intervention in the internal affairs of states has been increasingly relaxed. The UN subscribed to human rights early on, adopting the Universal Declaration of Human Rights in 1948; it has since been backed up by a range of more specific agreements and treaties, most notably the International Covenant on Civil and Political Rights. Member states that have ratified the treaties are obligated to respect and observe these rights. However, the enforcement mechanisms are still weak and often limited to monitoring systems. Possibilities for individuals to seek relief in case of violations are developing slowly on the global level.

Nevertheless, human rights have gradually been gaining priority over the classical principles of self-determination and nonintervention in states' internal affairs, including civil wars. Intervention was permitted by the UN Genocide Convention as early as 1948. Serious violations of human rights committed by states against individuals or groups are increasingly taken as justification for military intervention by outside states. Many of the details here are controversial: the compatibility of such actions with the UN Charter, the extent of human rights violations that justify humanitarian intervention, the proportionality requirements, and the like.

This is also true for the most recent development in international human rights law, the responsibility to protect the civilian population against serious violations of human rights. This responsibility was originally articulated by an expert group in 2001 and later adopted in a UN General

Assembly resolution as well as a Security Council resolution.[8] The primary addressees of this responsibility are the states, which must protect their own populations. But if states fail to fulfill this duty, the responsibility devolves upon the international community. No consensus has been reached as yet regarding a duty to intervene on the part of other states.[9]

In this context, a crucial role is played by the development of international courts. The International Court of Justice, the UN's judicial body, still operates entirely within the framework of classical international law and may only act if state parties have accepted its jurisdiction. But the international criminal tribunals for former Yugoslavia and Rwanda, which were not based on treaties among member states but on resolutions by the Security Council, could act without the agreement of the affected states, even on their territories and vis-à-vis their citizens.

Furthermore, under the influence of the UN, general international law is also changing in ways that have a limiting effect on sovereignty. Nontreaty international law remains customary law, but UN General Assembly resolutions have gained greater influence on the emergence of *opinio juris,* which is necessary for the formation of customary law. Within customary law, *jus cogens* is becoming more extensive; unlike other customary law, it cannot be waived by treaty, but in fact binds states in concluding treaties.[10]

Other international organizations also have a sovereignty-restricting effect. An important role is played by the World Trade Organization, founded in 1994.[11] The WTO has no rule-making powers but provides a forum for negotiations among member states aimed at multilateral agreements. As far as enforcement is concerned, however, the WTO has broken with the traditional international law model; it includes a courtlike institution, the Dispute Settlement Body, that can issue binding rulings in disputes over treaty violations and can impose severe sanctions.

That the UN's sovereignty-changing effects have not yet been fully appreciated results primarily from the fact that most states have not felt these effects acutely, since they give the UN no reason to intervene. UN interventions occur mainly in situations in which no state, or no effective state authority, remains; where various pretenders are fighting for state power; or where states themselves have become the perpetrators of grave violations of human rights or war crimes. This does not change the fact that the legal institution of external sovereignty is no longer identical with the traditional Westphalian order.

All this is, however, surpassed by regional developments in Europe. Following World War II, two forms of international cooperation emerged there: the Council of Europe, formed in 1949 by ten European states and now comprising forty-seven states, with the purpose of achieving "greater unity between its members for the purpose of safeguarding and realizing the ideals and principles which are their common heritage and facilitating their economic and social progress" (article 1 of the statute), and the European Union, founded by six countries in 1957 as the European Economic Community and since grown to encompass twenty-eight states and extend far beyond a common market.

Various agreements have been concluded by the states in the Council of Europe; they are not legislative acts of the Council of Europe itself, but remain entirely within the bounds of traditional international law. The most important treaty in regard to the sovereignty of the member states was the European Convention on Human Rights, adopted in 1950 and frequently amended. It is significant because of the body formed specifically to enforce it, the European Court of Human Rights; as a result of its powers, it ensures the convention far greater effectiveness than, for example, the human rights instruments of the UN or other regional covenants.

The European Convention on Human Rights departs from traditional concepts of sovereignty in two ways. First, it grants each member state the right to take another country's human rights violations before the court (article 33) and thus to intervene in its internal affairs. Second, it not only pertains to relations between states but also allows individuals to bring proceedings against member states for violations of the rights protected in the convention (article 34). While little use is made of the possibility of complaints by states,[12] the right of individual petition has become a widely used instrument.

But the traditional concept of international law remains untouched, insofar as the decisions of the European Court of Human Rights have no direct effect within the states. The court does not have the status of an appellate court. It is limited to determining convention violations by member states, but it cannot quash acts of the member states. They are obligated, under article 46, to obey the decisions of the European Court of Human Rights, but this is an obligation under international law. They cannot be forced to fulfill this obligation even by the Committee of Ministers, which is appointed to oversee compliance with the court's judgments.

In the European Union, in contrast, traditional international law categories prevail only in the field of intergovernmental cooperation. In the core areas of European integration, such as the Common Market, they no longer persist. It is still true that the legal basis of the European

Union is an international treaty between sovereign states and not a constitution. However, in concluding the treaties, the member states transferred sovereignty rights to the European Union, which the union now exercises in its own name and with direct effect within the member states. European law does not need to be transformed into domestic law, and its interpretation and application by the Commission and the European Court of Justice are binding on the member states.

It was not expected from the outset that European Community law would have this effect. The Treaty of Rome outfitted the European Community with legislative powers but left open the manner in which these legal norms would take effect. Possibilities included an international law method according to which member states would have been obligated to bring their domestic legal systems into conformity with the treaty, or a quasiconstitutional method, according to which the treaty provisions would take direct effect within the member states and enjoy primacy over domestic law so that the citizens could invoke them against their states. It took two groundbreaking decisions by the ECJ in favor of the second option to resolve the issue; they initiated the process that would later be understood as a "constitutionalization" of community law.[13]

It is true that the body primarily responsible for legislation is comprised of the governments of the member states, while the European Parliament has only a right of participation, generally confined to the veto. However, we must distinguish between the body and its members. The members, as representatives of their states, determine how the states will vote in the Council. But the decision itself is a decision by a European Union body and thus, for the member states, a heteronomous act. While the primary law of the European Union is international treaty law, its secondary law, based on this primary law, is European legislation.

However, the primacy of community law does not go so far as to cancel the validity of contrary national law, since we are speaking of two separate legal systems with independent sources of law. National law that contravenes community law does not lose effect simply because it is found to be incompatible with community law. However, as long as the community law obstacle exists, the contravening national law may not be applied. The effect is essentially the same. The only difference is that national law is immediately revived when contrary community law ceases to exist. The member states are still the "masters of the treaties," but they are no longer masters of the law that applies to their territories.

The only issues that remain controversial are whether this also applies to the core provisions of national constitutions that determine their very identities and who has final say in cases of doubt as to whether a legislative power has been transferred.[14] Aside from these reservations, the primacy of European law is uncontested, and it is applied by the member states as interpreted by the ECJ, which has freed itself largely from the methods of interpretation usual in international law and adopted a purposive approach common in national law. Yet since the European Union lacks a bureaucracy of its own in the member states, the implementation of EU law is left to the member states. Moreover, no member state has given up the monopoly of legitimate force, so that the union must rely on their coercive means in cases of noncompliance.

The consequences for the sovereignty of the member states long remained concealed, because until 1987 the Council of Ministers could only decide unanimously. Hence no member state had to submit to a European law without its consent. In addition, it went largely unnoticed that a second, clandestine way of enlarging the powers of the EU existed through the integration-friendly jurisprudence of the ECJ. In the meantime, however, majority voting has become the norm in the Council, so that the method of voting no longer assures that member states are only subject to rules to which their democratically elected and accountable representatives have agreed. Furthermore, the judicial activism of the ECJ has become a matter of public concern.[15]

Today, in foreign affairs, no state is sovereign in the sense in which states were sovereign in the nineteenth and even the first half of the twentieth century. This is clearly the case for the member states of the European Union. It is also true, however, for UN member states, and even more so for those that have ratified the treaty on the International Criminal Court. An exception may be made—not purely factual, but based on legal status—for states that do not belong to the European Union and hold a permanent seat on the UN Security Council, because no UN measures may be taken without their agreement. If they belong to the WTO, however, their sovereignty, too, has been compromised.

This has not ended the territorial linkage of political rule. States remain the basic units of the international order. But they are no longer the sole rulers on their territory. Instead, external acts of a legislative, administrative and judicial nature—often enacted with the cooperation of the affected states, but frequently without it—claim effect on this territory. The borders between states are not disappearing as a result, but they have become permeable and open to acts of external authority. The distinction between internal and external has become blurred. The state is changing in the same way. The twenty-first century state is different from the state in the Westphalian epoch.

Yet a distinction must be made between the horizontal and vertical dimension. A state's power to rule still ends at its own borders. No state has the right to govern another state. No state must submit to the rule of another. Externally based acts of rule emanate from international or supranational institutions, established and equipped with sovereign rights by states themselves, as a result of modern challenges and in order to increase their capacity to solve problems. The tasks of these institutions can be narrowly or broadly defined, but all are built upon states. None of them is capable of replacing the state.

As a result, a twofold picture emerges for external sovereignty. It retains its traditional meaning in the horizontal relationship between states. In the vertical relationship of states to international organizations, however, it has shrunk. This is true for all states, but not in the same way. The degree to which sovereignty is impaired depends, first, on the extent of sovereign rights acquired by the various international organizations and, second, on whether individual states have been granted veto rights in the statutes of international organizations. Thus what varies is the intensity with which sovereignty is impaired, but not the basic fact that sovereignty in the traditional sense has been lost.

3. EFFECTS ON INTERNAL SOVEREIGNTY

External and internal sovereignty may be distinguished, but not completely separated. It appears possible for a polity to be externally sovereign, even if there is no internal body that fully controls public power. This is the result of the fact that external sovereignty is linked solely to the existence of a state equipped with public power and is unaffected by questions regarding its internal allocation, separation, and limitation. To enjoy external sovereignty, it is sufficient that a state is capable of acting externally as a legal subject—though this ability, in turn, is not entirely independent of its ability to assert itself internally.

The converse is not the case, however; a polity cannot have internal without external sovereignty. If a political system loses its external sovereignty, it cannot maintain sovereignty internally. Lack of external sovereignty means nothing less than the subordination of state power to a foreign will and to that extent rules out self-determination. If the heteronomy were comprehensive, however, one would no longer be dealing with a state. The name *state* can only be claimed by an entity that retains powers that only it can exercise. This counts as sovereignty, however, only if it is based on a different concept of sovereignty than Bodin's.

The fact that external sovereignty does not simply shrink but is actively relinquished, through transfer of sovereign rights to international organizations of which the transferring state becomes a member, makes no difference to the result. Even if it is relinquished in an act of self-determination, the result is heteronomy. The superior entity gains the power to issue orders that bind the members and supersede their own legal acts. If this may happen without the agreement of the affected member, or even against its express will, its own will no longer matters. It is no longer sovereign in the traditional sense.

This is the fundamental difference between self-limitation without transfer of sovereign rights to a superordinate organization, as has always been common, and self-limitation with the transfer of sovereign rights to a superordinate political entity, which did not happen until the mid-twentieth century, except when individual sovereign states formed a federal state. The older self-limitation might lend treaty parties a legal claim to adherence to the limitation, but gave no possibility of one-sided command that might overrule an opposing will. Here, sovereignty asserts itself against international law.

This observation does not depend on who holds sovereignty internally. If a body exists that is viewed as sovereign, such as the British Parliament, on which British national law sets no boundaries, its sovereignty is over if an external body has the right to obstruct the national body's will or to prescribe decisions that it does not want to take. This situation emerged when the United Kingdom entered the European Community in 1972, while the Civil Rights Act of 1997, with which the European Human Rights Convention was adopted into national law, did not transgress the limits. The House of Lords admitted the loss of sovereignty in its decision in Factortame v. Secretary of State for Transport.[16]

This observation also affects states that are based on popular sovereignty, which is common today. Popular sovereignty is expressed in the act of constitution making. The constitution establishes the modalities by which the power to govern in the name of the people is granted and sets the conditions under which these powers may be exercised. The constitution's claim to validity is comprehensive. Acts of governance may only be enacted within its ambit by those legitimized by the constitution, and they can only be binding if they correspond to the formal and substantive rules provided for in the constitution.

In many states that are potentially but not actually subject to the decisions of international organizations, this continues to be the case, so that the limits on sovereignty are not perceptible. But it is not true for the member states of the European Union. In these states a variety of legal acts claims validity on a daily basis, the authors of which are not included in the web of legitimacy and responsibility provided for in the national constitutions; furthermore, they need not fulfill the procedural and substantive requirements that the constitutions establish for acts of public authority within their jurisdictions. The constitution as an expression of popular sovereignty applies only with reservations.[17]

It makes no difference that ever more national constitutions have authorized the transfer of sovereign rights to supranational institutions, and thus opened themselves up to acts of governance from supranational sources of law. Such authorizations prevent this situation from being unconstitutional. But they cannot change the fact that these constitutions no longer control the use the European Union makes of these transferred sovereign rights, leading to results that could not have withstood constitutional scrutiny, whether measures prohibited by the constitution must be taken or measures required by the constitution may not be taken. Even a loss of sovereignty that conforms to the constitution is still a loss of sovereignty.

So not all acts of public authority that claim effect within the ambit of a constitution can still be ascribed to the people, to whom sovereignty is attributed. The constitution ensures the observance of the will of the people only to the extent that the state power they legitimize and limit acts independently. The legitimating principle of popular sovereignty fails in the case of acts emanating from a supranational power. The constitution, as its mode of expression, now only partially regulates the political process. To the extent that it retreats, popular sovereignty can no longer claim effect.

A description of the current situation would be incomplete, however, if it ended with the assertion that states have surrendered sovereignty, in the traditional sense of full possession of the public power and sole disposal over the means of governance, and are thus no longer sovereign in the sense they were until the mid-twentieth century. The depiction must also include the fact that supranational organizations have not attained sovereignty. They possess only a more or less large number of sovereign rights. No supranational or international organization, including the European Union, has full possession of public power. None has achieved a monopoly of legal force within its ambit.

The fact that the new international order, in contrast to the state order, is structured not hierarchically, but heterarchically, leads to a system of mutual entanglement and dependence. In order to understand it, one must distinguish between the existence and legal basis of the entities, on the one hand, and the acts of governance that emanate from them, on the other. In regard to the existence and legal basis, states continue to be autonomous. They themselves decide upon the purpose and form of their political unity. This is also true for the member states of the European Union. Certain forms of constitution, such as those that undermine the rule of law, would make a state unsuited for membership. But this does not lend the European Union the power to determine the constitutions of its member states. At most, it can only deny membership.

In contrast, no international organization possesses self-determination regarding its own existence and legal basis—that is, sovereignty in the sense of the constituent power. International institutions are brought to life by states, which determine their basic legal orders, purposes and tasks, organs and instruments, powers and procedures. Their legal basis is externally determined and differs in precisely this way from the constitutions that are the legal bases of states. The fact that the legal bases of supranational institutions are increasingly referred to as "constitutions" means that, tacitly, an essential element of constitutionalism is being surrendered.[18]

The picture changes, however, if we move from the level of the basic order to that of action. While in traditional international organizations this level also remains the responsibility of the member states, that is no longer the case for the newer international systems to which states have transferred sovereign rights. If the transferred powers are exercised by an organ of one of these international institutions, it decides autonomously, even if the member states participate in the decisions as part of this organ. If its acts are directly binding on the member states, the states have lost the corresponding degree of self-determination.

The situation is equally unclear at the level of the judicial system, since it is not completely hierarchical, as it is in the state. Instead, competing jurisdictional claims are made by the European Court of Justice, on the one hand, and national supreme courts, on the other. National constitutional courts, in particular, insist on their right to review European Union acts for conformity with basic national rights and preservation of the powers not transferred to the European Union, while the ECJ contests that right. As long as no clear superior/subordinate relationship exists, there is no way to overcome this discrepancy. Thus the judicial system, too, depends on mutual deference.[19]

A picture therefore emerges of a mutual intermingling of autonomy and heteronomy, in which states sometimes act in self-determined fashion and international organizations are heteronomous, while at other times international organizations operate autonomously and states must allow external determination. The gap is never bridged through the ascription of the public power of international organizations to an equivalent of the people as bearers of sovereignty. Even the European Union has no such collective holder of its public power.[20] It is this observation that leads one to ask whether the concept of sovereignty still reflects reality and continues to be useful in portraying that reality, or whether we have entered a "postsovereignty" era.[21]

Sovereignty Today

The answer to these questions cannot be found in the history of the concept of sovereignty. As we have shown, no clear standard exists for applying the concept. The constellations to which it has referred are too different, the meanings it has taken on in fluctuating relationships and ideas too numerous, and the functions it has fulfilled at various times and in various places too uneven. But this does not render a historical examination unnecessary. Precisely because it reveals the variety of meanings, the context dependence and adaptability of the concept, such an examination prevents overhasty determinations and prognoses.[1] There are many gradations and combinations of conceptual elements between the medieval use of the word and the Hobbesian idea of sovereignty.

The number of works seeking an answer has grown apace.[2] We are facing a veritable sovereignty boom in the legal and political literature, such as only a crisis can generate. No consistent view has yet emerged. More and more authors advocate abandoning the concept because it has lost its object and is no longer helpful in explaining the current situation. In their view, all that remains is a variety of powers, distributed among several levels and holders, which can no longer be meaningfully bundled into a concept of sovereignty. Thus sovereignty would no longer serve its purpose as the key to understanding the state and the international order.

Yet declarations of the death of sovereignty, as history reveals, are nothing new. Earlier claims that the concept could not be reconciled with current ideas of legitimate political rule, or that the object it described had disappeared and therefore the concept itself had to be eliminated from the legal and political vocabulary, generally proved on closer examination to involve the disappearance of the conditions for a very specific concept of sovereignty. The same cannot be ruled out for the most recent diagnoses. Sovereignty deniers must therefore take a position on the possibility that the concept can be adapted to changed conditions or values without losing substance or function.

This seems all the more advisable since sovereignty continues to play an important role in domestic and international legal documents as well as in international relations. States raise and reject claims in the name of sovereignty, and international organizations are reluctant to deny states their sovereignty. The state of positive international law and political practice both lend sovereignty considerable resilience, which should not be ignored in scholarly works.[3] A number of authors have found it more important to develop a notion of sovereignty that meets present conditions and needs than to prove its obsolescence.[4]

The authors who take this path, hoping to adapt the concept of sovereignty to changing conditions, appear to be greater in number than the sovereignty deniers. Yet no consensus has been reached so far on explanations of the concept. However they would like to interpret sovereignty, sovereignty advocates must provide evidence that the concept still has explanatory value and fulfills a function that cannot be expressed by related concepts or those incorporating elements of sovereignty, such as public power, sovereign rights, self-determination, or the monopoly of force. Like the obsolescence of sovereignty, its continued value must be explained.

The task is made no easier by the fact that, in clarifying this question, a distinction must be made between the concept and its object. The object and the concept are neither unrelated nor identical. They are located on different levels: the object on the level of actual conditions, the concept on the level of the imagination of reality, its meaningfulness or value. Both are subject to change, but because of the different levels on which they operate the changes are not necessarily synchronous. The process of change can also be different at the same time, depending on the countries or regions or on academic and political trends.

Even if movements on the two levels are unsynchronized, they cannot remain completely independent of each other. This protects the use of the term from arbitrariness. The concept of sovereignty is certainly open to interpretation, depending on perception and assessment, but not to all interpretations simultaneously. What was always unique to it, even in its use before Bodin, was its quality as highest and ultimate authority regarding the right to make decisions and give orders that are binding on others. Sovereignty in its legal usage has a connection to rule, in the sense that it involves the *right* to rule, in which the holder of this right, as far as it extends, is controlled by no one else.

Bodin's contribution was to separate the concept of sovereignty from individual prerogatives or powers and to consolidate them into public power per se, including the right to make law, as well as the concentration of this power in one holder, thereby eliminating the numerous, mutually independent holders. Where this step toward uniformity and indivisibility was taken, the necessary result was the territorialization of rule. Because territorialization, together with concentration of force, ended in the emergence of the modern state system, the external independence of the state was implicit. The coexistence of various highest authorities with a claim to exclusivity was made possible by the territorial limitation of sovereignty.

Strictly speaking, a *concept* of sovereignty existed only from that point on. In its medieval usage, *sovereignty* was only a word used to describe specific positions of rule. As Reinhart Koselleck has explained in the introduction to his encyclopedia of basic historical terms, a concept is associated with a word, but is also more than that word. "A word becomes ... a concept when the abundance of a socio-political context of meaning, in which—and for which—a word is used becomes part of the word in its entirety."[5] This was the case with Bodin's theory: the word *sovereignty* now disclosed the character of a new system of rule, whereas the medieval world order could not have been subsumed under this expression.

However, the lack of substantive limits on the holder of this concentrated power was not an element of Bodin's notion of sovereignty. It was declared only later to be a marker of sovereignty and was never uncontested. Nor was sovereignty in Bodin's sense bound to a particular holder of political power. It is true that Bodin imagined the holder to be a person, so that holding and exercising sovereignty were joined. A single individual was not the only possible holder of sovereignty, however, but also a collective of people. Ascription of sovereignty to an abstract entity like the state was a product of later developments, however much Bodin's concept may have laid the groundwork for it.

An always controversial issue, answered in the negative by Bodin, was whether sovereignty is divisible. The most important reason for the persistence of this issue was the variation in the political structures of the territories that lagged behind France in concentrating power, or simply refused to do so, but could not escape the pull of the concept of sovereignty. One could be called sovereign even if one was not the sole possessor of public power. Either a bundle of sovereign rights was enough upon which to base sovereign status, or it had to be recognized that several holders could cooperate in exercising sovereignty, so that none of them alone was supreme.

The most successful way to deal with this difficulty was to depersonalize the holder of sovereignty. The concentration and uniformity of public power, in contrast to the separation of sovereign rights, could be maintained if sovereignty was ascribed to the state that thereby became a legal person. The depersonalized holder of sovereignty, it is true, was no longer able to exercise the powers linked to it by itself, but had to utilize persons or groups of persons that acted as its organs. The state itself was but the entity to which sovereignty was ascribed and symbolized the unity of the sovereign rights exercised separately by the various branches of government.

This solution was not available, however, for federal entities—in particular for federal states—because federal states are constituted from individual states; therefore the distribution of state power cannot be limited to the level of its exercise, but extends to the level of the holder. The federal state thus remained a constant source of irritation for the doctrine of sovereignty. Yet it was the actual existence of federal states that forced a deeper reflection on sovereignty and produced a significant number of variants of the concept—some of them monist, some dualist. Given the distribution of sovereign rights between states and international organizations, these variants have gained renewed significance today.

With the emergence of the constitutional state, the step to depersonalization of sovereignty was complete. When fully formed, it could recognize only democracy as the legitimating principle for political rule. Sovereignty thus meant popular sovereignty. The people were not capable of acting politically, however. Sovereignty therefore found expression only in the act of constitution making. The powers connected with sovereignty were exercised by delegates or representatives as derived powers. This made it easier to reconcile sovereignty with limitations of power, because the limitation took place only below the level of sovereignty, at the level of its exercise.

Something similar is now happening at the international level. An international legal order is emerging that no longer depends exclusively on self-determination by states but is imposed on them regardless of their consent. To this extent, parallels may be observed with the constitution-alization of state power, which likewise occurred as a transition from self-limitation by the absolute ruler to a limitation on political rule by way of legal norms emanating from a source other than the ruler and not at his disposal.[6] This parallel is the backdrop to the ubiquitous discussion on the constitutionalization of international law, even if it tends to neglect the significant differences between a full-fledged constitution and the present state of international law.

Nevertheless, it is becoming clear that the development encapsulated in the notion of constitutionalization far exceeds prior alterations of sovereignty, because recent developments concern the territoriality of political rule. They present a much more severe challenge to sovereignty because they involve the external self-determination of states, fundamen-tally untouched for centuries, and thus necessarily narrow their internal self-determination. This plays out most strongly in the European Union, where the opening of the member states to legal acts emanating from nonstate sources has progressed the farthest. However, the union itself has not become a superstate, which would have led the sovereignty dis-cussion back to the familiar question of the federal state.

The Westphalian order of territorially limited states in full possession of public power within their borders, and protected against external claims to rule, is being replaced by an as yet unclear framework in which the condensed public power exercised by the state is again split into its components, individual sovereign rights. These rights—some as larger or smaller bundles, some as individual powers—are exercised by various holders, neither clearly equal nor clearly hierarchically structured, and are applied in part functionally, in part territorially, and at times once again displaced onto new agencies within existing authorities such as the European Monetary Union or the Schengen Agreement.

This raises the question whether we have returned to a pre-Bodin state of affairs and therefore can now only employ the medieval concept of sovereignty. However, one difference is immediately apparent. While the Middle Ages saw only the first signs of state formation, the states in this post-Westphalian world continue to form the fundamental units of the newly emerging order. Even if they are no longer in full possession of the public power that operates on their territory, they are the source of supranational power and hold the majority of sovereign rights. This is also true of the members of the European Union.

If we ignore this difference and look only at the supranational level, then the individualization of the sovereign rights exercised there, and their distribution among many mutually independent holders, may recall medieval conditions. But in this regard, too, the differences are significantly greater than the parallels. In the Middle Ages the juxtaposition of a large number of holders of personally oriented, functionally limited powers of rule resulted in a comprehensive system of rule. In contrast, the institutions that may exercise international public power today rise like islands from a sea in which, as before, traditional states predominate, though reduced to the extent of the rights they have transferred to supranational actors.

Additionally, the medieval holders of sovereign rights were bound to a comprehensive legal order that, at least in its foundations, was considered God-given and therefore sacrosanct. This legal order allocated to each his position and his rights and duties within the overall order. The order itself was overarching, and decentralized only in its preservation and implementation. In contrast, international law is fragmented and broken up into a range of unconnected legal regimes—trade, environmental protection, human rights, migration, and so forth—whose agents operate not in concert, but separately and committed to their specific agenda, so that often the allocation of a problem to a particular regime determines in itself in whose favor it will be resolved.[7]

Thus medieval analogies do not help in understanding the present. Today's reality is too strongly affected by modern concepts of sovereignty, and too permeated by current claims to sovereignty, for the recent conceptual tradition to be laid aside. Nor, however, can it be maintained unchanged. The characteristics that have become questionable are in fact those that, until recently, were considered fundamental. "If one understands sovereignty," Laband taught, "as the supreme, highest, only self-determined power, this concept logically includes the characteristic of unlimitedness, and consequently also the characteristic of indivisibility," for division meant limitation and would be "a complete contradictio in adjecto."[8]

If the unlimited nature of the right to rule were necessary to the concept of sovereignty, no sovereignty would be left today. Political rule, in terms of its purposes and means, has long been limited in the constitutional state, as well as more recently under international law. Even the constituent power that sets the limits of state power in the constitution is no longer sovereign, in the sense of completely unlimited freedom, although this absolute freedom is still maintained in the concept of popular sovereignty. A constitution that, for example, deprived a certain group of people of all rights would violate international law and, if enforced, could justify intervention.

The situation is similar, though more complicated, for indivisibility. Given the transfer of sovereign rights to the supranational level, sovereignty would be at an end if the only way to define it were the concentration of all public powers in one place. The states have lost the monopoly of public power, but no supranational organization has gained it.[9] If the concept of sovereignty is to continue to be applicable, it must be separated from the full possession of public power. This can happen by reducing the standard of indivisibility or accepting divisibility or developing a different concept of sovereignty. All three methods have been attempted.

The indivisibility of sovereignty, under today's changed conditions, can be maintained only if a distinction is made between abstract sovereignty and concrete sovereign rights. Such attempts can be observed in the European discourse on sovereignty.[10] Some authors insist on the indivisibility of sovereignty, but do not consider it to be affected by the distribution of sovereign rights. The only controversial point, as in German constitutional law after the founding of the Reich, is who is sovereign, the European Union or the member states. Although the issue at the time was only the location of sovereignty in the (federal) state, while today sovereignty is debated in connection with a supranational institution, the arguments are similar.

Advocates of member-state sovereignty rely on the source of the primary law of the European Union, which is adopted by unanimous decision of the member states. They remain the "masters of treaties" and, according to the principle of conferral, retain the legislative *Kompetenz-Kompetenz*. Advocates of European Union sovereignty rely on the effect of community law, which enjoys primacy over national law—even the highest-level national law, the constitution—and on the power of the

ECJ to decide conflicts about the distribution of competences, which gives it the so-called judicial *Kompetenz-Kompetenz.*

But only the two points of view together yield the full picture. The state-friendly alternative ignores the fact that, within the scope of European Union powers, states are prevented from making their own decisions and are subject to external decision making. The fact that they may participate, at least in legislative decisions by the Council, does not change this; it does not guarantee that their wishes will be implemented by the community bodies. The European Union–friendly alternative overlooks the fact that the European Union is not the master of its own legal basis—it has no right of self-determination in that respect—and that the ECJ's right of final decision in conflicts of authority is controversial.[11]

This unitary thesis recently gained strong support, in its state-friendly variant, from the Federal Constitutional Court of Germany. Sovereignty played a crucial role in its Lisbon judgment, in contrast to the Maastricht decision.[12] The difference was expressed in the court's statement that the Basic Law not only presumes sovereign statehood but guarantees it. The court did distance itself from a "rigid" interpretation of sovereignty, which is not compatible with the transfer of sovereign rights to supranational institutions; it distinguished between sovereign rights and sovereignty. Membership in a political union such as the European Union means the common exercise of certain public powers, not divided sovereignty.

The boundary, and therefore the fundamental difference, between the member states and the union as a nonstate entity is self-determination regarding the constitutional basis of the political entity. Sovereignty is expressed primarily in the constituent power. While the member states possess this power, the European Union does not. It cannot constitute itself. Its basic order is derived from the states. They remain the masters of the treaties. In a confederation there is no shift of sovereignty.[13] Nor is there an independent popular sovereignty belonging to citizens of the Union as a whole, but only European representation by individual nations at the level of community bodies, below the level of sovereignty.[14]

Germany's right of self-determination, guaranteed by sovereignty, is not, however, limited to the constituent power. It continues on the level below the constitution, in political decision making. There, too, the Federal Republic must retain substantive opportunities for decision making. The German Constitutional Court listed matters it considered "sensitive" for a constitutional state's ability to structure itself and that therefore could not be transferred completely to the European Union. Even less may the European Union avail itself of these powers. The principle of conferral is constitutive for the protection of the sovereignty of the member states.

Derived from this is the idea that the primacy of community law over national law is treaty based and not inherent in community law. The national constitution allows it to be applied domestically. If this permission has not been given, European law is not applicable in Germany. Moreover, because sovereignty remains in the hands of the member states, they cannot be denied the right to review European laws and legal acts as to their conformity with treaties. This review power, which the Constitutional Court earlier claimed for conflicts over basic rights, on the model of the Solange II judgment,[15] as well as for "deviating acts," has now been extended to the constitutional identity of the Basic Law.

By claiming the judicial *Kompetenz-Kompetenz* in these matters, the German Constitutional Court avoided leaving gaps in its arguments for sovereignty, which would be the case if the European Court had the last word in conflicts of authority. In that case, the German Constitutional Court would no longer be able to stop expansions of union power through treaty interpretations that might amount to treaty amendments. The position of the member states as "masters of the treaties" would thus lose value. With the judicial *Kompetenz-Kompetenz,* claims of sovereignty remain coherent and can only be attacked by questioning their premises.

The Constitutional Court found the basis for this view in the principle of democracy, which is indissoluble under article 79(3) of the Basic Law, as long as the Basic Law is in force. The Court interpreted democracy as self-determination regarding a state's own basic order, as well as political decision making within this basic order by organs that act at the behest of the people and are accountable to them. It saw the member states as a "constituted primary political sphere" that is protected in its substance by the Basic Law. Sovereignty's task is to guarantee national democracy. The Constitutional Court is authorized to give effect to this guarantee.

The European Court maintains the opposite view. It does not deny the member states' sovereignty, but starts with the assumption that a part of it has been transferred to the European Union, including the right of final decision in conflicts over authority. The fact that the Union's legal basis consists of international treaties in which the member states are the masters is a more difficult obstacle to overcome. The Court has attempted to clear this hurdle by looking beyond member states as treaty parties and ascribing treaties to the peoples of the member states in order to provide them with a normative authority independent of the states. This system also seems to be open to question only on its premises.

Oliver Beaud has proposed an unconventional solution to the problem of sovereignty in federally organized political entities. Federations, in his view, cannot be comprehended using the concept of sovereignty. He gave the corresponding chapter in his book the title "Setting Aside Sovereignty to Conceptualize Federalism."[16] Sovereignty cannot be divided and is therefore reserved to states. A federation, in contrast, is "a political order without sovereignty."[17] In consequence, a federally organized entity cannot be a state. Beaud indeed comes to this conclusion and develops new rules for such an entity's external relations, alongside international law, which is reserved for relations between sovereign states.

In order to hold on to sovereignty, numerous authors avoid these difficulties by abandoning the element of indivisibility. They accept a "pooled, shared, divided, split or partial sovereignty" ("divisibility, alienability, compossibility and mixity") for the newly emerging international order,[18] as well as for the special case of the European Union. In this view, there may be several sovereigns on one and the same territory. If sovereigns are still to be characterized by the fact that they have no one above or next to them, this is only possible if final say is limited to their respective areas of authority—that is, each holder of sovereignty is only the highest "in his sphere," as Waitz expressed it.

In fact, when dealing with the possibility of divided sovereignty today, some observers are once again invoking Waitz and earlier German constitutional law doctrine, which was superseded soon after the foundation of the Reich by constitutional positivism and its rigid concept of sovereignty.[19] For an older generation, the federal state was characterized more by the equal relationship of its members than by hierarchical relations. Federal powers and the powers of the individual states had to be independent, Waitz wrote, "The former may not receive its power from the latter, and the latter may not be based on a transfer of power from the former."[20] A division of sovereignty is more easily reconciled with this than with a hierarchical concept of national unity.

However, the older doctrine took shape around the idea of a federally organized nation. Therefore, it is not clear that it applies to the relationship between states and supranational organizations as well as it does to different members within a nation-state. In contrast to nation-states, which as a rule are not merely alliances of convenience but communities of solidarity based on common traditions and values, international organizations generally pursue limited goals and therefore do not produce deep bonds in the population. This makes it doubtful that a concept of sovereignty based on belonging can be transferred to them.

Furthermore, in contrast to territorially limited states, which have retained, even in the post-Westphalian order, a large majority of public tasks and public power, supranational organizations are typically functionally limited, often in the interests of a single task, and—to the extent they are equipped with any public power—only possess the powers necessary to fulfill that task. No supranational organization has yet been granted the right to use physical coercion. States continue to hold the monopoly of legitimate force. When supranational organizations depend on the use of force to implement their measures, they must engage the states.[21]

This is true even for the United Nations. If it wishes to intervene militarily in the interests of maintaining peace or protecting human rights, it must borrow troops from cooperating states. The European Union, too, with its comparatively greater breadth of functions and organizational density, and corresponding powers, has no coercive apparatus of its own. If its measures can only be enforced through physical force, it depends on the coercive apparatuses of member states. It might issue legal provisions for their use, to a limited extent. But it cannot give them any orders.

One may still ascribe sovereignty to states despite the loss of unlimited self-determination. But this is much more difficult for supranational entities that only have enumerated tasks and can use public power only to the extent necessary to fulfill these tasks. And, except for the European Union, this is not how these organizations see themselves. If supranational organizations, with their limited tasks and related powers, were sovereign, this would in fact resemble an unspecific, premodern concept of sovereignty in which it is enough for someone to exercise various prerogatives as a final arbiter.

If sovereignty, therefore, even under today's conditions, requires that a political entity not only exercise a special function with related sovereign rights, but that it possess a broader set of tasks with the corresponding range of public powers, then it is at least imprecise to speak generally of divided sovereignty in the relationship between states and supranational organizations. Divided sovereignty means that each side possesses a piece of sovereignty and not merely some of the sovereign rights that, in their entirety, used to comprise sovereignty. The sovereign rights that have been surrendered do not, as a rule, consolidate back into (partial) sovereignty in the supranational organizations.

The European Union falls into another category, however. In its number of tasks, range of powers, and organizational density, it outstrips all other supranational organizations, without having crossed the threshold to a federal state. Therefore those who believe that one cannot do justice to the new circumstances using monist concepts of sovereignty with the mere division of sovereign rights, but only through the divisibility of sovereignty itself, find their most convincing case in the European Union.

Nevertheless, one would hesitate to use the term *sovereign* to refer to a political entity that does not possess the right of self-determination regarding its existence, purpose, powers, and organization. As mentioned before, this is the case with the European Union. Sovereignty means, among other things, self-determination, albeit within legal limits, but the European Union lacks constituent power. As far as its legal foundation is concerned, it is heterodetermined. It therefore seems incorrect to characterize the European Union as a political entity with divided sovereignty.

Is it at least correct then to speak of pooled or shared sovereignty, meaning that the nation-states united in the European Union exercise their sovereignty jointly within or through the union? This may have seemed to be the case in the early years of European integration, when European decision making required unanimity among the member states. Meanwhile, however, the European Union has become an entity that may act independently of its member states, though with binding effect on them. A member state that receives an order from the European Union does not obey the other member states, but the European Union.

There is, however, no necessity for sovereignty to persist. Neil MacCormick's "post-sovereignty" is not an impossibility, certainly not in Europe. Rather, one might imagine a situation in which sovereignty will be completely absent in the European Union. This could happen if the member states either transferred or lost so many powers that those remaining would no longer deserve to be called sovereign, but without the European Union gaining constituent power. This situation would not be identical with Schmitt's suggestion that, in a *Bund*, the sovereignty question is left open. Rather, the sovereignty question would no longer be posed within the European Union, while sovereignty might survive in the external relations of the union and its member states.

However, the European Union has inspired still other ideas of how the concept of sovereignty can be adapted to the new situation by renewing its meaning. They employ labels such as "constitutional pluralism," "late sovereignty," and "contrapunctual law"[22] and start with the premise "that no unitary approach, however nuanced, can adequately capture the diversity of the emerging constitutional order." Therefore, a fourth way must be found that overcomes the dualism of state and nonstate, original and derived powers, constitution and treaty, superior and subordinate, in favor of a concept that avoids renewed unity formation or hierarchization, but also fragmentation of political authority.

The difference from the divisibility and the indivisibility theories is that these authors recognize the sovereignty claims of both sides, take seriously their inherent demands for exclusivity, and do not resolve them in favor of one side but concede sovereignty to both sides, the union and the member states. Since sovereignty always involves the highest ordering power and preservation of identity, it includes an "irreducible core, the non-negotiable given of any sovereign order." Neither side may demand preference for its sovereignty claims from the other. Each must allow the other to count. "Identity is lost if it is not self-determined."[23]

The union and the member states, along with their courts, are forced in this way to enter into dialogic rather than confrontational methods of settling conflicts, which Neil Walker considers necessary to his concept of "constitutional pluralism." If none can trump the others by appealing to its own sovereignty, the only remaining possibility is to negotiate opposing standpoints. Because the issue is ultimately about defending identity, however, the theory factors in the possibility that negotiation may not succeed and tensions must be tolerated. Such is the cost of abandoning attempts at hierarchy, which can only be avoided if the European Union transforms into a federal state.

This indicates that today, too, the possibility of adapting the concept of sovereignty to changed conditions exists. There is, however, no absolute necessity to stick to sovereignty, for instance in order to prevent anarchy. Since sovereignty is not identical with political rule, but represents a particular form of political rule, its absence cannot be equated with civil war or anarchy. It is true that modern sovereignty formed in order to overcome civil wars. But anarchy did not prevail in the presovereign world; nor would the postsovereign world have to descend into anarchy. Effective political rule is indispensable, but it does not need to be imagined as sovereign.

Nor does basing powers of rule in the people depend on sovereignty. It is common to describe constitution making as an act of sovereignty originating with the people, who can at any time take up this power again. To this extent, it may be said that the sovereignty absent in the constitutional state withdraws into the people's constitution-making authority. But the people are only capable of acting after having been constituted as a political entity by the constitution, and then, like the various branches of government, act only as bearers of specific powers, not bearers of the constituent power. The locus of this sovereignty remains fictional, as does sovereignty itself.

This is not an argument against popular sovereignty as the basis of political rule. But popular sovereignty does not involve sovereignty in the sense of the highest, irresistible power. Rather, it comes into play in its capacity as a legitimizing principle for rule determined by the constitution. It indicates that political rule can be legitimized not by an original right of the ruler, nor by divine law, nor by superior insight into the common good, and certainly not by the mere control of the means of force, but only by popular mandate, and can only be exercised with responsibility toward the people. Everything achieved by popular sovereignty as a principle for legitimizing and organizing political rule is expressed in the concept of democracy.

In contrast, where it refers to the external dimension, the concept of sovereignty cannot simply be replaced. In political rhetoric, the concept of sovereignty is, anyway, omnipresent. But in the scholarly literature, too, the tendency to abandon "sovereignty" is generally weaker than the disposition to retain the concept, though perhaps with a change in meaning. These changes even sometimes take up traditional elements accompanying the history of the concept. The absolute nature of sovereignty was never uncontested. Its plausibility was generally limited to historical situations involving extreme threats to a polity. Without such a situation, the need to legally limit even the highest, irresistible power regularly came to the fore.

When its unlimited nature was asserted, this was largely irrelevant to the actual exercise of rule, either because sovereignty was pushed into the constituent power or was ascribed to an abstract entity that only became capable of action through its organs, which were not omnipotent. Self-limitation was the means through which the unlimited nature of the right to rule could be reconciled with the limitation of its exercise. The same result was achieved by the distinction between possessing and exercising sovereignty. But there was always a concept of sovereignty that was legally limited from the outset.

Divisibility also had an older tradition, generally forced by the structure of the political system, in the form of either a distinction between sovereignty and sovereign rights or a distribution among various holders, each one of which had pieces of sovereignty at its disposal or could only take advantage of undivided sovereignty in cooperation with the others. Even an unbridgeable dualism, as has been proposed in the most recent suggestions for adapting sovereignty to the European situation, was thought earlier in history to be reconcilable with sovereignty. What is new is the international constellation, not the repertoire for dealing with it.

In a political world whose basic units continue to be the states, external sovereignty is not simply brought along as an obsolete relic. It is still more or less obvious. The boundaries between states, and therefore their claims to territorial exclusivity, may have been relativized in a way that makes an absolute concept of sovereignty seem implausible. But the boundaries have by no means dissolved; even in the European Union they largely retain their earlier significance in the horizontal dimension—that is, in the relationship of states among themselves. They are porous in the vertical dimension—that is, in the relationship of states to international organizations and their laws and military actions—but, even there, only occasionally.

As far as the evidence of sovereignty is concerned, it must always be kept in mind that interventions by the organized international community, the United Nations and functionally specialized institutions like the WTO, remain only potential for most states and are seldom or never actualized. For failed or fragmented states, or for rogue states, the impact of international missions on their territory can be quite severe; but the purposes of these missions are temporary and aimed at the restoration of functioning states. Therefore, in the world outside Europe, sovereignty has far greater plausibility than in integrated Europe. It is still perceptible and more or less effective.

It would therefore be wrong to assess the conditions under which sovereignty continues to be possible from only the European perspective. The European Union is a special case in comparison with the rest of the world. Nowhere has the traditional interpretation of sovereignty been so strongly challenged. But this special status would disappear if the European Union were to be transformed into the United States of Europe. Also, in terms of quantity, the special European case does not carry much weight. The member states of the European Union make up less than 15 percent of all the states in the world. Incidentally, on its outer borders and in the relationship of the member states to nonmember states, the usual conditions prevail.

The fact that, given this reality, it is not implausible to continue to think in terms of sovereignty with regard to foreign policy does not mean that the function of sovereignty must remain the same. Whenever sovereignty is invoked, power claims are at stake. These claims are addressed to those who are supposed to accept and respect them. Inherent in this observation is the idea that all claims to sovereignty have their opponents. They can refuse any rule that is based on sovereignty. They can also combat the prevailing interpretation of sovereignty by disputing its justification or proposing a different meaning. The history of sovereignty is filled with such debates.

For this reason, the actual lines of conflict deserve attention. Many older differences have paled over time. This is especially true for the opposition between absolute and limited sovereignty. At least to the extent that constitutionalism has prevailed, this dispute has been decided in favor of the latter. Controversy continues over the divisibility of sovereignty. However, this conflict has weakened considerably through the understanding that sovereign *rights* can be distributed among various holders. This also eliminates the conflict between an abstract, unitary concept and a concrete plural concept of sovereignty. The question, therefore, is what is being defended and contested when claims of sovereignty are raised.

There is much evidence that the lines of conflict at present run mainly between particular and cosmopolitan norms, democratic self-determination in state-organized entities and claims to universal validity of moral postulates, "new sovereigntists" and "internationalists."[24] Among the cosmopolitan norms, human rights stands out. In contrast, external sovereignty took its meaning from the outset from the self-determination of states. It guaranteed internal sovereignty. It is true that in the constitutional state sovereignty has retreated into the constituent power, but this leaves the right of external self-determination unaffected. It continues to be guaranteed to states, due to their sovereignty, and includes, in particular, decisions on the foundations and design of the political system.

Human rights movements frequently view sovereignty as morally unacceptable because it places national interests above universal values. Indeed, the protective wall sovereignty placed around the self-determination of states was originally impenetrable. International law recognized only states as legal subjects. How they acted on their own territory was a domestic matter, regulated by national law, but uninteresting for international law. Human rights could not be asserted at the international level. One of the greatest changes in the postwar era, however, is that this concept of sovereignty is disappearing.

International law now penetrates state borders and also applies to the relationship between states and their inhabitants. To a limited degree, these inhabitants also gain international legal subjectivity, specifically as possessors of human rights, which are now internationally guaranteed. Even military interventions by the international community are accepted to protect human rights.[25] Essentially, states can no longer claim sovereignty as a defense against humanitarian intervention. This development is new, and its details are still unsettled. In principle, however, the opposition between sovereignty and human rights has been overcome. The right of self-determination no longer covers violations of international humanitarian law.

Some authors find it insufficient, however, to understand human rights as mere limitations on sovereignty. They advocate subordinating sovereignty to human rights. Accordingly, conflicts between sovereignty and human rights would be solved not by balancing, but with a presumption in favor of human rights. Sovereignty would thus lose its status as a first principle of international law and would be replaced by a new normative foundation that is no longer centered on the state. Instead, the whole system of international relations would be centered on the individual. This does not mean that states would disappear. But they would be entitled to invoke the sovereign right of self-determination only insofar as it would serve individual well-being. This concept is presented under the heading of "humanization of sovereignty" or "humanized sovereignty."[26]

Yet individual well-being is always realized in a community—a collective entity that is more than the sum of its individual members and that has developed a collective identity distinguishing it from other communities. Even if a community shares the view that the well-being of its individual members is the ultimate goal, there will always be different opinions about the meaning of well-being. A consensus that individual well-being depends on the recognition of human rights may narrow the area of controversy but does not eliminate it. Even in this case, the scope and range of human rights and the best way to accommodate conflicting rights are controversial issues and thus require political decisions.

The primary space for making these collectively binding decisions is still the state. International law protects the right of states to make these decisions according to their rules and preferences. The same is true for a nation's choice of its political system. One may be convinced that the most favorable environment for human rights is a democratic system, because only in a democracy do individual citizens have a chance to participate in collective decision making in a meaningful way. But it would be difficult to argue that democracy is a necessary precondition of human rights. Certainly, no state is obliged by international law to organize itself in a democratic fashion.

If "humanized sovereignty" meant that only political systems that combine human rights with democracy could enjoy sovereignty, many states would lose the legal protection of self-determination. Depriving them of sovereignty in this sense might be regarded as an invitation for all sorts of interventions by other states. For this reason, the idea of replacing sovereignty with human rights as the highest principle of international law has met with considerable criticism.[27] Even a proponent of "humanized sovereignty," Anne Peters, admits that the principle of self-determination should "still be understood to protect the capacity to choose a political system commensurate with one's national culture, even if this results in an illiberal and authoritarian regime."[28] And humanized sovereignty is still sovereignty.

Yet human rights are threatened not only by states but also by international organizations. Most international organizations, even if charged with the protection of human rights, are not themselves bound by these rights. At a time when the impact of international organizations is growing, it is a serious postulate that they, too, should be obligated to respect and not only protect human rights.[29] The same is true with regard to self-determination. It can also be threatened by international organizations, if they succumb to institutional self-interest or allow themselves to serve the interests of certain states. Power is prone to misuse, whether in the hands of states or of international institutions.

Democracies are dependent, to a particularly great extent, on states' right to self-determination because democratic principles currently find the best conditions for their realization in the context of the state. The more ambitious the concept of democracy, the less likely it is to be realized beyond the state.[30] Democracy should not be reduced to periodic elections. Rather, elections will fulfill their function only if they are embedded in a constant process of opinion formation and articulation of interests. This is a demanding process dependent on mediation by parties, associations, and the media, which provide for constant feedback between the government and the governed, even between elections. Political participation works more or less well within the framework of the state, while it is increasingly diluted the more international organizations depart from the state level.

For now, democratic self-determination still depends largely on the state. This is true in relation not only to global but also to regional institutions. The laws and orders of the European Union are heteronomous acts from the perspective of the member states, if they have not agreed to them or have had no opportunity to participate in them, because their representative, the Council, had no say in the decision-making process. This is the case, for example, when the union takes away from member states the right to decide which areas to leave to market regulation and which to regulate publicly, in the interest of compensating for market failures.

The Lisbon judgment of the German Constitutional Court was based on these considerations. It defended the sovereignty of the Federal Republic not in the interests of the nation-state but in the interests of democracy,[31] which enjoys better conditions in the nation-state than in the European Union and under article 79(3) of the Basic Law cannot be relinquished. It also did not defend it against European integration, which is not only permitted by the Basic Law but, according to the Court, even required. The Court thus also did not deny the primacy of community law, but defended it against the danger of depletion through overeager surrender and creeping deprivation of powers.

Apart from that, the defense is confined to threats to the identity of the state's constitutional order. The judgment contains no statement regarding the incompatibility of European secondary law with the treaties. This is reserved for the European Court of Justice, which is the authentic interpreter of the treaties. The German Constitutional Court limited itself to determining under what conditions, according to German constitutional law, European legal acts could not apply on the territory of the Federal Republic. It is the authentic interpreter of the Basic Law. This should be compatible with the "fourth way" advocated by Walker and other authors.

Sovereignty's most important function today lies in protecting the democratic self-determination of a politically united society with regard to the order that best suits it. The progressive supranational fulfillment of public tasks that exceeds the abilities of individual states, as well as the further juridification of internationally exercised public power, are not hindered by this developing concept of sovereignty. As long as there is no convincing model of a global democracy, the source of democratic legitimacy and supervision must not run dry at the state level. Today sovereignty protects democracy.

Notes

SERIES EDITOR'S FOREWORD

1. A more detailed historical-political account of the issues treated in these early phases of Grimm's more conceptual-legal analysis (which also treats the French revolution) can be found in Dick Howard, *The Primacy of the Political* (2011), published also in the series *Political Thought/Political History*.

2. The reader may recognize similarities to Claude Lefort's theory of democracy as based on the "empty place of power." For Lefort, this leads to what he called (in a volume published in this series in 2007) Complications in the analysis of the new world that came into being after the complications" the Fall of the Wall. I think that Dieter Grimm would accept the description.

A. SOVEREIGNTY IN A TIME OF CHANGING STATEHOOD

1. Jean Bodin, *Six Books of the Commonwealth* (Oxford: Blackwell, 1967 [1576]).

2. Hugo Preuss, *Gemeinde, Staat, Reich als Gebietskörperschaften* (Berlin: J. Springer, 1889); Léon Duguit, *Law in the Modern State* (New York: B. W. Huebsch, 1919 [1913]); Hans Kelsen, *Das Problem der Souveränität und die Theorie des Völkerrechts* (Tübingen: Mohr, 1920); all discussed in Hermann Heller, *Die Souveränität* (Berlin: Walter de Gruyter, 1927), 19ff.

3. Georg Jellinek, *Allgemeine Staatslehre* (Berlin: O. Häring, 1900), quoted here from the seventh reprint of the third edition (1914), published by Walter Jellinek (Darmstadt: Wissenschaftliche Buchgesellschaft, 1960), 435; see also Quentin Skinner, "The Sovereign State: A Genealogy," in Hent Kalmo and Quentin Skinner, eds., *Sovereignty in Fragments: The Past, Present and Future of a Contested Concept* (Cambridge: Cambridge University Press, 2010), 1; see also ibid., 26.

4. See Ulrich Haltern, *Was bedeutet Souveränität?* (Tübingen: Mohr Siebeck, 2007).

5. Juliane Kokott, "Die Staatsrechtslehre und die Veränderung ihres Gegenstandes in Veröffentlichungen der Vereinigung der deutschen Staatsrechtslehrer," *VVDStRL* 63 (2004), 19.

6. See Paul W. Kahn, "The Question of Sovereignty," *Stanford Journal of International Law* 40 (2004): 259; Haltern, *Was bedeutet Souveränität?*

1. BODIN'S SIGNIFICANCE
FOR THE CONCEPT OF SOVEREIGNTY

1. On the emergence and early significance of "sovereignty," see Marcel David, *La souveraineté et les limites juridiques du pouvoir monarchique*

du IXe au XVe siècle (Paris 1954); Jürgen Dennert, *Ursprung und Begriff der Souveränität* (Stuttgart: Gustav Fischer, 1964); Otto von Gierke, *Johannes Althusius und die Entwicklung der naturrechtlichen Staatstheorien*, 4th ed. (Breslau: Marcus, 1929), 123ff.; Francis H. Hinsley, *Sovereignty* (New York: Basic Books, 1966); Gaines Post, *Studies in Medieval Legal Thought: Public Law and the State, 1100–1322* (Princeton: Princeton University Press, 1964); Helmut Quaritsch, *Souveränität: Entstehung und Entwicklung des Begriffs in Frankreich und Deutschland vom 13. Jh. bis 1806* (Frankfurt: Duncker & Humblot, 1986); Saskia Sassen, *Territory, Authority, Rights: From Medieval to Global Assemblages* (Princeton: Princeton University Press, 2006); Helmut G. Walther, *Imperiales Königtum, Konziliarismus und Volkssouveränität: Studien zu den Grenzen des mittelalterlichen Souveränitätsgedankens* (Munich: Fink, 1976); Michael Wilks, *The Problem of Sovereignty in the Later Middle Ages* (Cambridge: Cambridge University Press, 1963).

2. Jean Bethke Elshtain, *Sovereignty: God, State, and Self* (New York: Basic Books, 2008), 1ff., 29ff.

3. "Chaque Baron est souverain dans sa baronnie." Philippe de Beaumanoir, *The Coutumes de Beauvaisis of Philippe de Beaumanoir* (Philadelphia: University of Pennsylvania Press, 1992 [1842]), ch. 34, §1043, 368.

4. Joseph R. Strayer, *On the Medieval Origins of the Modern State* (Princeton: Princeton University Press, 1970), 91; see also 9, 36.

5. See Quaritsch, *Souveränität*, 35.

6. The claim is made by Hendrik Spruyt, *The Sovereign State and Its Competitors: An Analysis of Systems Change* (Princeton: Princeton University Press, 1994), 38; in contrast, see Otto Brunner, *Land*

und Herrschaft: Grundfragen der territorialen Verfassungsgeschichte Österreichs im Mittelalter, 6th ed. (Darmstadt: Wissenschaftliche Buchgesellschaft, 1970), 141f.

7. See, e.g., Walter Ullmann, *Papst und König: Grundlagen des Papsttums und der englischen Verfassung im Mittelalter* (Salzburg: Pustet, 1966), 26f., and *The Growth of Papal Government in the Middle Ages: A Study in the Ideological Relation of Clerical to Lay Power* (London: Methuen, 1955), 276ff., 414ff.

8. See Brunner, *Land und Herrschaft.*

9. Of the wealth of literature on Bodin, see especially Olivier Beaud, *La puissance de l'Etat* (Paris: Presses universitaires de France, 1994), 47ff.; Jean-Jacques Chevallier, *Les grandes oeuvres politiques,* 9th ed. (Paris: Colin, 1966), 38; William F. Church, *Constitutional Thought in Sixteenth Century France: A Study in the Evolution of Ideas* (Cambridge: Harvard University Press, 1941); Horst Denzer, ed., *Jean Bodin: Verhandlungen der internationalen Bodin-Tagung in München* (Munich: Beck, 1973); Julian H. Franklin, *Jean Bodin and the Rise of Absolutist Theory* (Cambridge: Cambridge University Press, 1973); J. U. Lewis, "Jean Bodin's 'Logic of Sovereignty,'" *Political Studies* 16 (1968): 206; Quaritsch, *Souveränität;* Quentin Skinner, *The Foundations of Modern Political Thought* (Cambridge: Cambridge University Press, 1978), 2:284ff.

10. See Skinner, *The Foundations of Modern Political Thought,* 254ff.

11. Michel de l'Hôpital, *Oeuvres complètes,* ed. P. J. S. Duféy (Geneva: Slatkine, 1968), 1:449f.; Bernard de Girard Haillan, *De l'Etat et succès des affaires de France* (Paris, 1611), 1; see Skinner, *The Foundations of Modern Political Thought,* 349ff., and *Visions of Politics* (Cambridge:

Cambridge University Press, 2002), 2:368ff.; H. C. Dowdall, "The
Word 'State,'" *Law Quarterly Review* 39 (1923): 98; Paul Ludwig
Weinacht, *Staat, Studien zur Bedeutungsgeschichte des Wortes von
den Anfängen bis ins 19: Jahrhundert* (Berlin: Duncker & Humblot,
1968); Brunner, *Land und Herrschaft*; Ernst Wolfgang Böckenförde,
"Die Entstehung des Staates als Vorgang der Säkularisation," in Ernst
Wolfgang Böckenförde, *Recht, Staat, Freiheit* (Frankfurt: Suhrkamp,
1991), 92; Strayer, *On the Medieval Origins of the Modern State.*

12. Skinner, *The Foundations of Modern Political Thought,* 285ff.

13. See Roman Schnur, *Die französischen Juristen im konfessionellen
Bürgerkrieg des 16. Jahrhunderts* (Berlin: Duncker & Humblot, 1962);
Skinner, *The Foundations of Modern Political Thought,* 249ff.

14. Jean Bodin, *Six Books of the Commonwealth* (Oxford: Blackwell, 1967
[1576]), book 1, ch. 8, 32, 28.

15. Ibid., book 6, ch 1.

16. "Les loix . . . ne dependent que de sa pure et franche volonté." Ibid.,
book 1, ch. 8.

17. "If the prince can only make law with the consent of a superior he
is a subject; if of an equal he shares his sovereignty; if of an inferior,
whether it be a council of magnates or the people, it is not he who is
sovereign." Ibid., book 1, ch. 10, 43.

18. Ibid., book 3, ch. 5, 92.

19. Ibid., book 1, ch. 8, 31, book 3, ch. 4, 89. On deconfessionalization, see
Quaritsch, *Souveränität,* 387.

20. Many authors see in this merely inconsistency or even confusion,
e.g., George H. Sabine, *A History of Political Theory,* 3d ed. (London:
Harrap, 1963), 408; a different interpretation can be found in Qua-

ritsch, *Souveränität*, 52f., 60ff.; Skinner, *The Foundations of Modern Political Thought*, 294ff.

21. "Fausse et nulle." Bodin, *Six Books*, book 3, ch. 4, 86.

22. See, e.g., Strayer, *On the Medieval Origins of the Modern State*. 91.

23. Listed in Denzer, *Jean Bodin*, 494–96.

24. See Georg v. Below, *Der deutsche Staat des Mittelalters*, vol. 1, 2d ed. (Leipzig: Quelle & Meyer, 1925); Heinrich Mitteis, *Der Staat des hohen Mittelalters*, 6th ed. (Weimar: Böhlau, 1959). See also Brunner, *Land und Herrschaft*, 146ff.

25. See Ulrike Krautheim, *Die Souveränitätskonzeption in den englischen Verfassungskonflikten des 17. Jh: Eine Studie zur Rezeption der Lehre Bodins in England von der Regierungszeit Elisabeths I. bis zur Restauration der Stuartherrschaft unter Karl II* (Frankfurt: Peter Lang, 1977).

26. Quoted in William Holdsworth, *A History of English Law*, 3d ed. (London: Sweet and Maxwell, 1945), 5:451, note 2; George L. Mosse, *The Struggle for Sovereignty in England* (East Lansing: Michigan State University Press, 1950), 133.

27. See Michael Stolleis, *Geschichte des öffentlichen Rechts in Deutschland* (Munich: Beck, 1988), 1:170ff.; Gierke, *Johannes Althusius*, 164ff.; Rudolf Hoke, "Bodins Einfluss auf die Anfänge der Dogmatik des deutschen Reichsstaatsechts," in Denzer, *Jean Bodin*, 315, and "Mais qui était donc le souverain du Saint Empire?" *Revue d'histoirie des facultés de droit et de la science juridique* 19 (1998): 5.

28. Bodin, *Six Books*, book 1, ch. 9, 40, book II, ch. 6, 70.

29. See Dietrich Reinkingk, *Tractatus de regimine secularies ecclesiastico* (Giessen: Hampel, 1619).

30. See Johannes Limnäus, *Dissertatio apologetica de statu Imperii Romano-Germanici* (Ansbach: Lauer, 1643).

31. Hugo Grotius, *De iure belli ac pacis* (Paris, 1625); Samuel Pufendorf, *De iure naturae et gentium* (Paris: Buon, 1625 / Lund: Junghans, 1672).

32. Skinner, *The Foundations of Modern Political Thought*, 338; Gierke, *Johannes Althusius.*

33. Thomas Hobbes, *Leviathan*, in *The Clarendon Edition of the Works of Thomas Hobbes,* ed. Noel Malcolm (Oxford: Clarendon, 2012), vol. 3, chapter 18.

34. Ibid.

35. Particularly developed in Skinner, *Visions of Politics,* 368ff.

36. John Locke, *The Second Treatise of Government,* in *The Works of John Locke Esq* (London: John Churchill, and Sam. Manship, 1714), vol. 2, ch. 11, 134ff. Locke reached this result by assuming, unlike Hobbes, that the ruler obtained his authority not from a social contract among individuals but from a second contract between the people and the ruler.

37. See Diethelm Klippel, *Politische Freiheit und Freiheitsrechte im deutschen Naturrecht des 18. Jahrhunderts* (Paderborn: Schöningh, 1976).

38. Jean-Jacques Rousseau, *The Social Contract,* ed. Maurice Cranston (London: Penguin, 1968), book 1, ch. 6, 60.

39. Ibid., book 3, ch. 15, 141.

2. SOVEREIGNTY IN THE CONSTITUTIONAL STATE

1. Emer de Vattel, *The Law of Nations* (Philadelphia: Johnson, 1849 [Emer de Vattel, *Le droit des gens ou principes de la loi naturelle,*

Leiden: Aux Depens De La Compagnie, 1758]), § 27. See Heinz Mohnhaupt and Dieter Grimm, *Verfassung: Zur Geschichte des Begriffs von der Antike bis zur Gegenwart*, 2d ed. (Berlin: Duncker & Humblot, 2002), 91, 105; see also Hasso Hofmann, *Politik—Recht— Verfassung: Studien zur Geschichte der politischen Philosophie* (Frankfurt: Hermann Luchterhand, 1986), 277f.

2. See Dieter Grimm, *Die Zukunft der Verfassung*, 3d ed. (Frankfurt: Suhrkamp, 2002), 31ff. The English unwritten "constitution" is evidence of this; see 51f., 75ff.

3. Gordon S. Wood, *The Creation of the American Republic, 1776–1787*, 2d ed. (Chapel Hill: University of North Carolina Press, 1998), 345, see also 354.

4. Samuel Johnson, "Taxation No Tyranny," in *American Archives*, 4th series, 1:1431f.

5. William Blackstone, *Commentaries on the Laws of England* (Oxford: Clarendon, 1765), 1:48f. On its reception in America, see Arthur E. Sutherland, *The Law at Harvard* (Cambridge: Belknap, 1967), 24f.

6. Declaration of Colonial Rights and Grievances of the First Continental Congress, October 1, 1774; Declaration of Independence of July 4, 1776, both in Henry Steele Commager, ed., *Documents of American History*, 9th ed. (Englewood Cliffs: Prentice Hall, 1973), nos. 56 and 66.

7. See Wood, *The Creation of the American Republic*, 393ff., and especially 403ff.

8. Vattel, *The Law of Nations*, book 1, ch. 1, § 6, 3.

9. See Wood, *The Creation of the American Republic*, 403ff.

10. See Bruce Ackerman, *We the People* (Cambridge: Belknap, 1998), 2:32ff., 2:49ff.

11. See Wood, *The Creation of the American Republic*, pp. 469ff., 519ff.; Ackerman, *We the People*, 1:216ff.

12. *The Federalist*, no. 78. On *The Federalist*, see Ackerman, *We the People*, 1:165ff.

13. See Wood, *The Creation of the American Republic*, 472f.

14. Edmund S. Morgan, *Inventing the People: The Rise of Popular Sovereignty in England and America* (New York: Norton, 1989), 267.

15. See Akhil Reed Amar, *America's Constitution* (New York: Random House, 2006), 28ff.

16. Ibid., 308ff.

17. See Pierre Rosanvallon, *La démocracie inachevée: Histoire de la souveraineté du peuple en France* (Paris: Gallimard, 2000).

18. Ibid., 14ff.

19. Emmanuel Joseph Sieyes, "What Is the Third Estate?" in Michael Sonenscher, ed., *Political Writings* (Indianapolis: Hacket, 2003 [1789]). See Jean-Jacques Chevallier, *Les grandes oeuvres politiques*, 9th ed. (Paris: Colin, 1966), 174; Pasquale Pasquino, *Sieyès et l'invention de la constitution en France* (Paris: Jacob, 1998); Olivier Beaud, *La puissance de l'Etat* (Paris: Presses Universitaires de France, 1994), 223ff.; Egon Zweig, *Die Lehre vom pouvoir constituant: Ein Beitrag zum Staatsrecht der französischen Revolution* (Tübingen: Mohr, 1909).

20. See Guillaume Bacot, *Carré de Malberg et l'origine de la distinction entre souveraineté du peuple et souveraineté nationale* (Paris: CNRS, 1985), 117ff.

21. Benjamin Constant, "Principles of Politics Applicable to All Representative Governments," in *Constant: Political Writings*, ed. Biancamaria Fontana (Cambridge: Cambridge University Press, 1988), 177.

22. Raymond Carré de Malberg, *Contribution à la Théorie générale de l'Etat*, 2 vols. (Paris: Librairie de la Société du recueil Sirey, 1920), 1:69ff.; 2:152ff., 167ff. See Bacot, *Carré de Malberg;* Stéphane Pierré-Caps, *Nation et peuple dans les Constitutions modernes* (Nancy: Presses universitaires de Nancy, 1990).

23. Carré de Malberg, *Contribution à la Théorie générale de l'Etat*, 2:483ff.

24. "Il résulte de là que la formation intitiale de l'Etat, comme aussi sa première organization, ne peuvent être considérée que comme un pur fait, qui n'est susceptible d'être classé dans aucune catégorie juridique, car ce fait n'est point gouverné par des principes de droit." Ibid., 490f.

25. "Il n'y a dans l'Etat que des organes constitutés." Ibid., 500.

26. "Elle se ramêne a une question de fait et cesse d'être une question de droit." Ibid., 497.

27. "Du plus fort." Ibid., 496.

28. "Le pouvoir qui appartient à la nation d'exprimer et d'imposer sa volonté par ses organs réguliers." Ibid., 539.

29. "Entraîne, comme consequence nécessaire, la séparation du pouvoir constituant." Ibid., 548.

30. See Michel Troper, *Terminer la Révolution: La Constitution de 1795* (Paris: Fayard, 2006), 109ff.

31. See, e.g., Francis Hamon and Michel Troper, *Droit constitutionnel*, 28th ed. (Paris: LGDJ, 2003), 177ff.; Jacques Ziller, "Sovereignty in France," in Neil Walker, ed., *Sovereignty in Transition* (Oxford: Hart, 2003), 261.

32. Décision 92–313 DC.

33. See Dieter Grimm, *Deutsche Verfassungsgeschichte*, 3d ed. (Frankfurt: Suhrkamp, 1995).

34. Art. I, Vienna Final Act, May 15, 1820; see also article 2 of the Confederate Act of June 8, 1815.

35. "Since the German Confederation, with the exception of the free cities, consists of sovereign princes, the entire authority of the state must, according to the basic concepts provided thereby, remain united within the head of state, and a constitution [*landständische Verfassung*] can bind the sovereign to the cooperation of the estates [*Mitwirkung der Stände*] only in the exercise of certain rights."

36. Johann Caspar Bluntschli, "Souveränität," in Johann Caspar Bluntschli and Karl Brater, eds., *Deutsches Staats-Wörterbuch* (Leipzig: Expedition d. Staatswörterbuches, 1865), 9:553.

37. Romeo Maurenbrecher, *Grundsätze des heutigen deutschen Staatsrechts* (Frankfurt: Varrentrap, 1837); Wilhelm Eduard Albrecht, *Rezension über Maurenbrechers Grundsätze des heutigen Staatsrechts*, Göttingische Gelehrte Anzeigen (Göttingen: Verlag der privilegiirten Universitets-Buchhandlung, 1837), 1489ff., 1508ff. See Walter Pauly, *Der Methodenwandel im deutschen Spätkonstitutionalismus* (Tübingen: Mohr, 1993), 23ff., 66 f., 77ff.

38. See Grimm, *Deutsche Verfassungsgeschichte*, 110–43.

39. Quaritsch, *Souveränität*, 498.

40. Georg Wilhelm Friedrich Hegel, *Grundlinien der Philosophie des Rechts* (Berlin: Nicolai, 1821), 279.

41. See Ulrich Häfelin, *Die Rechtspersönlichkeit des Staates* (Tübingen: Mohr, 1959); Pauly, *Der Methodenwandel*, 77ff.

42. See Paul Laband, *Das Staatsrecht des Deutschen Reiches* (Tübingen: Mohr, 1876), quoted here from the fourth edition (1901), 1:87.

43. Georg Jellinek, *Allgemeine Staatslehre* (Berlin: O. Häring, 1900), 552f.

44. H. Krabbe, *Die Lehre der Rechtssouveränität: Beitrag zur Staatslehre* (Groningen: Wolters, 1906); revisited by R. M. MacIver, *The Modern State* (Oxford: Clarendon, 1926), 467ff., 479.

45. Hans Kelsen, *Allgemeine Staatslehre* (Berlin: Springer, 1925), 93ff., especially 102ff.

46. Alexis de Tocqueville, *Democracy in America* (University of Chicago Press: Chicago, 2000 [1835]), 1:105.

47. *The Federalist*, no. 9.

48. See Jackson Turner Main, *The Antifederalists: Critics of the Constitution, 1781–1788* (Chapel Hill: University of North Carolina Press, 2004). On the following, see Richard Ellis, *The Union at Risk: Jacksonian Democracy, States' Rights, and the Nullification Crisis* (New York: Oxford University Press, 1987).

49. Speech on January 21, 1830, *Register of Debates in Congress*, 6:41.

50. Speech on January 26 and 27, 1830, in *The Works of Daniel Webster* (Boston: Little, Brown, 1853), 3:270; the quote is on 321.

51. Nullification Ordinance, quoted in Harry Williams, Richard N. Current, and Frank Freidel, *A History of the United States* (New York: Knopf, 1960), 1:372.

52. Speech on February 15 and 16, 1833, in *The Works of John C. Calhoun* (New York: Appleton, 1853), 2:197–262.

53. John Calhoun, "A Discourse on the Constitution and the Government of the United States," ibid., 1:146.

54. Ibid., 2:201.

55. Speech on February 16, 1833, in *The Works of Daniel Webster*, 3:448; the quotes are on 452, 465, 469, 477.

56. Speech on February 26, 1833, in *The Works of John C. Calhoun*, 2:262–309.

57. Ibid., 289f.

58. Chisholm v. Georgia, 2 U.S. (2 Dall.) 419 (1793): "Every State in the Union in every instance where its sovereignty has not been delegated to the United States, I consider to be as completely sovereign, as the United States are in respect to the powers surrendered. The United States are sovereign as to all the powers of Government actually surrendered. Each State in the Union is sovereign as to all the powers reserved." The decision on the distribution of powers among the courts was later overtaken by the Eleventh Amendment to the U.S. Constitution. As for today, see, e.g., U.S. Term Limits, Inc. v. Thornton, 514 U.S. 779 (1995): "Federalism was our Nation's own discovery. The Framers split the atom of sovereignty"; Printz v. U.S., 521 U.S. 898 (1997): "It is incontestable that the Constitution established a system of 'dual sovereignty.'"

59. See Alfred Koelz, *Neuere Schweizerische Verfassungsgeschichte* (Bern: Stämpfli, 1992), 1:543ff.; Eduard His, "Amerikanische Einflüsse im schweizerischen Verfassungsrecht," in *Festgabe zum Schweizerischen Juristentag 1920* (Basel: Helbing & Lichtenhahn, 1920), 81ff.

60. Franz Wigard, *Stenographischer Bericht über die Verhandlungen der deutschen constituirenden Nationalversammlung zu Frankfurt am Main* (Frankfurt: Sauerländer, 1848–49), 1:17.

61. Georg Waitz, "Das Wesen des Bundesstaats," *Allgemeine Monatsschrift für Wissenschaft und Literatur* (1853), 494; see also his *Grundzüge der*

Politik (Kiel: E. Homann, 1862), 153, in debate with Joseph Maria Radowitz's work of the same name, *Gesammelte Schriften,* vol. 2 (Berlin: Georg Reimer, 1852).

62. See Joseph Maria Radowitz, *Berlin und Erfurt,* in Radowitz, Gesammelte Schriften (Berlin: Reimer, 1852), 2:98ff.

63. Heinrich von Treitschke, *Aufsätze, Reden und Briefe* (Meersburg: Hendel, 1929), 3:38.

64. Max Seydel, "Der Bundesstaatsbegriff," *Zeitschrift für die Gesamte Staatswissenschaft* 28 (1872): 185–256 (on Calhoun, see 208–24), all following cites found here. See also the later works, specifically "Die neuesten Gestaltungen des Bundesstaatsbegriffs," *Hirth's Annalen* (1876), 641 (also in Max von Seydel, *Staatsrechtliche und politische Abhandlungen* (Freiburg: Mohr, 1893), 101.

65. An overview in the Reich is offered especially by Albert Hänel, *Deutsches Staatsrecht* (Leipzig: Duncker & Humblot, 1892), 1:200ff.; Hermann Rehm, *Allgemeine Staatslehre* (Freiburg: Mohr, 1899), 86–146; Laband, *Das Staatsrecht des Deutschen Reiches,* 1:51ff.; Georg Meyer and Gerhard Anschütz, *Lehrbuch des deutschen Staatsrechts,* 7th ed. (Leipzig: Duncker & Humblot, 1914), 11ff., 41ff., 121ff., 193ff., 224ff. A contemporary doctrinal history is found in Siegfried Brie, *Der Bundesstaat: Eine historisch-dogmatische Untersuchung* (Leipzig: W. Engelmann, 1874). Later, see Josef L. Kunz, "Die Staatenverbindungen," in *Handbuch des Völkerrechts* (Stuttgart: W. Kohlhammer, 1929), 2.4.21ff., 61ff., 595ff.; Michael Dreyer, *Föderalismus als ordnungspolitisches und normatives Prinzip: Das föderative Denken der Deutschen im 19. Jahrhundert* (Frankfurt: Lang, 1987); Michael Stolleis, *Geschichte des öffentlichen Rechts in Deutschland* (Munich: Beck,

1992), 2:365; Dieter Grimm, "Was the German Empire a Sovereign State?" in S. O. Müller and C. Torp, eds., *Imperial Germany Revisited: Continuing Debates and New Perspectives* (New York: Berghahn, 2011), 51.

66. Laband, *Das Staatsrecht des Deutschen Reiches,* 1:68.

67. Heinrich von Treitschke, "Bund und Reich," in Treitschke, *Aufsätze, Reden und Briefe,* 4:218ff.

68. Philipp Zorn, *Das Staatsrecht des Deutschen Reiches* (1880), 1:46ff., 84f., and "Neue Beiträge zur Lehre vom Bundesstaat," *Annalen des Deutschen Reichs für Gesetzgebung, Verwaltung und Statistik* (1884), 425.

69. Laband, *Das Staatsrecht des Deutschen Reiches,* 1:60ff., 67.

70. Georg Jellinek, *Die Lehre von den Staatenverbindungen* (Vienna: A. Hölder, 1882) and *Allgemeine Staatslehre,* 461ff., 474ff., 737ff. See also Jens Kersten, *Georg Jellinek und die klassische Staatslehre* (Tübingen: Mohr Siebeck, 2000), especially 294ff., 414ff.

71. Max von Seydel, *Kommentar zur Verfassungsurkunde für das Deutsche Reich,* 2d ed. (Freiburg: Mohr, 1897), 8.

72. Jellinek, *Die Lehre von den Staatenverbindungen,* 41ff. See also Heinrich Rosin, "Souveränetät, Staat, Gemeinde, Selbstverwaltung: Kritische Begriffstudien," *Annalen des Deutschen Reichs für Gesetzgebung, Verwaltung und Statistik* (1883), 265–322; Siegfried Brie, "Die Lehre von den Staatenverbindungen," *Grünhut's Zeitschrift* 11 (1888): 94ff.

73. Jellinek, *Allgemeine Staatslehre,* 475ff. The criticism is found especially in Rosin, "Souveränetät, Staat, Gemeinde, Selbstverwaltung," 265, and Brie, "Die Lehre von den Staatenverbindungen," 185.

74. Jellinek, *Allgemeine Staatslehre,* 481.

75. Ibid., 495f.

76. Albert Hänel, *Studien zum deutschen Staatsrecht*, 2 vols. (Leipzig, 1873), 1:63ff., 1:240; see also his *Deutsches Staatsrecht*, 73ff.

77. Kelsen, *Allgemeine Staatslehre*, 198ff.

78. "The 'organic ties' that an organization and its own organs are lacking . . . this common state that stands next to the individual state, for which however neither territory nor subjects remain . . . all these are not clear, definite legal terms." Laband, *Das Staatsrecht des Deutschen Reiches*, 81.

79. Kelsen, *Allgemeine Staatslehre*, 199.

80. Ibid., 200.

81. Carl Schmitt, *Constitutional Theory*, trans. Jeffrey Seitzer (Durham: Duke University Press, 2008), 388ff, a translation of his *Verfassungslehre* (Berlin: Duncker & Humblot, 1928), 370ff.

82. See part C.

83. On this characteristic, see Dieter Grimm, "Ursprung und Wandel der Verfassung," in Josef Isensee and Paul Kirchhof, eds., *Handbuch des Staatsrechts der Bundesrepublik Deutschland,* 3d ed. (Heidelberg: Müller, 2003), 1:25; Dieter Grimm, "Die Verfassung im Prozess der Entstaatlichung," in Peter M. Huber, Michael Brenner, and Markus Möstl, eds., *Der Staat des Grundgesetzes—Kontinuität und Wandel: Festschrift für Peter Badura zum siebzigsten Geburtstag* (Tübingen: Mohr Siebeck, 2004), 145; the English translation may be found in 12 *Constellations* 447 (2005); Dieter Grimm, "Types of Constitutions," in Michel Rosenfeld and Andras Sajo, eds., *The Oxford Handbook of Comparative Constitutional Law* (Oxford: Oxford University Press, 2012), 98. On the difference between the achievement of the

constitution, in the sense of a sophisticated constitutional concept, in contrast to a reduced one, especially in connection with the so-called European constitution, see Dieter Grimm, *Braucht Europa eine Verfassung?* (Munich: Carl Friedrich von Siemens Stiftung, 1995), "The Achievement of Constitutionalism and Its Prospects in a Changed World," in Petra Dobner and Martin Loughlin, eds., *The Twilight of Constitutionalism?* (Oxford: Oxford University Press, 2010), 3, and "Entwicklung und Funktion des Verfassungsbegriff," in T. Cottier and W. Kälin, eds., *Die Öffnung des Verfassungsrechts: Symposium zum 65. Geburtstag von J. P. Müller Recht* 2005 Sonderheft, Bern, 7–10.

84. See Beaud, *La puissance de l'Etat,* 201ff.; Jürgen Habermas, *Faktizität und Geltung* (Frankfurt: Suhrkamp, 1992), 170; Hasso Hofmann, *Das Recht des Rechts, das Recht der Herrschaft und die Einheit der Verfassung* (Berlin: Duncker & Humblot, 1998), 25; Martin Kriele, *Einführung in das Staatslehre: Die geschichtliche Legitimitätsgrundlagen des demokratischen Verfassungsstaats* (Reinbek: Rowohlt, 1975), 111ff.; Neil MacCormick, *Questioning Sovereignty* (Oxford: Oxford University Press, 1999), 129; Klaus Stern, *Das Staatsrecht der Bundesrepublik Deutschland* (Munich: Beck, 1980), 2:527ff.

85. Déc. 76–71 DC of December 29–30, 1976, Recueil des Décisions du Conseil constitutionnel; Déc. 92–308 DC of April 9, 1992, Recueil 55. "Transferts de competences," and "conditions essentielles d'exercice de la souveraineté nationale." Jean Combaçau, "La souveraineté internationale de l'État dans la jurisprudence du Conseil constitutionnel français," *Cahiers du Conseil constitutionnel* n° 9 (Dossier : Souveraineté de l'Etat et hiérarchie des normes)—février 2001.

86. BVerfGE 89, 155 (1993), 186ff.

87. BVerfGE 123,267 (2009), 343ff. See Dieter Grimm, "Defending Sovereign Statehood Against Transforming the European Union Into a State," 5 *European Constitutional Review* 353 (2009).

88. For trenchant commentary, see, e.g., Jed Rubenfeld, "Unilateralism and Constitutionalism," *New York University Law Review* 79 (2004): 1971; Jeremy A. Rabkin, *Law Without Nations? Why Constitutional Government Requires Sovereign States* (Princeton: Princeton University Press, 2005); an overview in Lars Viellechner, "Amerikanischer Unilateralismus als Verfassungsfrage," *Der Staat* 45 (2006): 1.

89. See Beaud, *La puissance de l'Etat,* 307 ff.

90. See Dieter Grimm, "Missglückt oder glücklos? Die Weimarer Verfassung im Widerstreit der Meinungen," in Heinrich August Winkler, ed., *Weimar im Widerstreit* (Munich: Walter de Gruyter, 2002), 151.

91. See Ulrich Haltern, "Tomuschats Traum," *Völkerrecht als Wertordnung: Festschrift für Christian Tomuschat* (Kehl: Engel, 2006), 877, 889.

92. On the effect of fictions, see Morgan, *Inventing the People,* 23ff. and elsewhere.

93. Carl Schmitt, *Political Theology: Four Chapters on the Concept of Sovereignty,* trans. Carl Schwab (Chicago: University of Chicago Press, 2006 [1922]), 5.

94. Ibid., 19.

95. Ibid., 13, 18.

96. See Dieter Grimm, "Verfassungserfüllung –Verfassungsbewahrung—Verfassungsauflösung: Positionen der Staatsrechtslehre in der Staatskriese der Weimarer Republik," in Heinrich-August Winkler, ed., *Die deutsche Staatskrise 1930–33: Handlungsspielräume und Alternativen* (Munich: Oldenbourg, 1992), 183.

3. EXTERNAL SOVEREIGNTY

1. See Saskia Sassen, *Territory, Authority, Rights: From Medieval to Global Assemblages* (Princeton: Princeton University Press, 2006); Michael Stolleis, "Die Idee des souveränen Staates," *Der Staat*, supplement 11 (1996): 63, esp. 67.

2. See, e.g., Jermias. E. Linck and Roland T. Diederich, *Dissertatio de civibus et peregrinis* (Strasbourg: Argentorati, 1729).

3. See Luzius Wildhaber, "Sovereignty and International Law," in Luzius Wildhaber, *Wechselspiel zwischen Innen und Aussen* (Basel: Helbing und Lichtenhahn, 1996), 19.

4. See Wilhelm Grewe, *Epochen der Völkerrechts-Geschichte* (Baden-Baden: Nomos Verlagsgesellschaft, 1984), 30f., 57ff.

5. Michael Stolleis, *Geschichte des öffentlichen Rechts in Deutschland* (Munich: Beck, 1988), 1:279.

6. Martti Koskenniemi, *The Gentle Civilizer of Nations: The Rise and Fall of International Law, 1870–1960* (Cambridge: Cambridge University Press, 2002).

7. See Andreas L. Paulus, *Die internationale Gemeinschaft im Völkerrecht: Eine Untersuchung zur Entwicklung des Völkerrechts im Zeitalter der Globalisierung* (Munich: Beck, 2001); Bardo Fassbender, "Sovereignty and Constitutionalism in International Law," in Neil Walker, *Sovereignty in Transition* (Oxford: Hart, 2003), 115.

8. International Commission on Intervention and State Sovereignty, *The Responsibility to Protect* (Ottawa: International Development Research Centre, 2001); UN, *A More Secure World: On Shared Responsibilities: Report of the Secretary General's High-level Panel on Threats, Challenges and Changes* (New York: United Nations, 2009);

UN General Assembly resolution of October 24, 2005 (UN Doc A/ RES/60/1); UN Security Council resolution of April 28, 2006 (UN Doc S/RES/1674).

9. See Theresa Reinold, *Sovereignty and the Responsibility to Protect: The Power of Norms and the Norms of the Powerful* (New York: Routledge, 2012); J. Holzgrefe and R. O. Keohane, eds., *Humanitarian Intervention: Ethical, Legal and Political Dilemmas* (Cambridge: Cambridge University Press, 2003); Gareth Evans, "Rethinking Humanitarian Intervention," *Proceedings of the American Society of International Law*, 98th annual meeting (2004), 78.

10. See Christian Tomuschat, "Obligations Arising for States Without or Against Their Will," *RdC* 241 (1993): 195; Christian Tomuschat and Jean-Marc Thouvenin, eds., *The Fundamental Rules of the International Legal Order: Jus Cogens and Obligations Erga Omnes* (The Hague: Martinus Nijhoff, 2006).

11. See Deborah Z. Cass, *The Constitutionalization of the World Trade Organization: Legitimacy, Democracy and Community in the International Trading System* (Oxford: Oxford University Press, 2005); John H. Jackson, *Sovereignty, the WTO, and Changing Fundamentals of International Law* (Cambridge: Cambridge University Press, 2006).

12. Overview in Mark Eugen Villiger, *Handbuch der Europäischen Menschenrechtskonvention*, 2d ed. (Zurich: Schulthess, 1999), marg. no. 118ff.

13. Van Gend and Loos, Slg. 1963, 1; Costa v. ENEL, Slg. 1964, 1253. On constitutionalization, see esp. J. H. H. Weiler, *The Constitution of Europe* (Cambridge: Cambridge University Press, 1999), 12 and elsewhere.

14. See BVerfGE 89, 155 (1993)—Maastricht Treaty; more recently, BVerfGE 123, 267—Lisbon Treaty.

15. See, e.g., Ulrich Haltern and Andreas Bergmann, eds., *Der EuGH in der Kritik* (Tübingen: Mohr Siebeck, 2012); Dieter Grimm, "Die Rolle der nationalen Verfassungsgerichte in der europäischen Demokratie," in Claudio Franzius, Franz C. Mayer, and Jürgen Neyer, eds., *Grenzen der europäischen Integration?: Herausforderungen an Recht und Politik* (Baden-Baden: Nomos, 2014), 14.

16. Factortame v. Secretary of State for Transportation, A.C. 603 (1991), esp. 658f.

17. See Dieter Grimm, "Zur Bedeutung nationaler Verfassungen in einem vereinten Europa," in Detlef Merten and Hans-Jürgen Papier, eds., *Handbuch der Grundrechte in Deutschland und Europa* (Heidelberg: C. F. Müller, 2009), VI/2:3.

18. See Dieter Grimm, "Ursprung und Wandel der Verfassung," in Josef Isensee and Paul Kirchhof, eds., *Handbuch des Staatsrechts der Bundesrepublik Deutschland,* 3d ed. (Heidelberg: Müller, 2003).

19. See Stefan Oeter and Franz Merli, "Rechtsprechungskonkurrenz zwischen nationalen Verfassungsgerichten, Europäischem Gerichtshof und Europäischem Gerichtshof für Menschenrechte," *Veröffentlichungen der Vereinigung der Deutschen Staatsrechtslehrer* 66 (2007): 361ff., 392ff.; Dieter Grimm, "La cour européene de justice et les jurisdictions nationale, vue sous l'angle du droit constitutionnel allemande," *Cahiers du Conseil Constitutionnel* 4 (1998): 70.

20. BVerfG 123, 267 (2009). Dieter Grimm, "Wer ist souverän in der Europäischen Union," in Dieter Grimm, *Die Zukunft der Verfassung* II (Berlin, 2012), 275; but see Jürgen Habermas, *Zur Verfassung Europas* (Berlin: Suhrkamp, 2011), 48ff.

21. See Neil MacCormick, *Questioning Sovereignty* (Oxford: Oxford University Press, 1999), 123ff.

1. See Quentin Skinner, "The Sovereign State: A Genealogy," in Hent Kalmo and Quentin Skinner, eds., *Sovereignty in Fragments: The Past, Present and Future of a Contested Concept* (Cambridge: Cambridge University Press, 2010).

2. A selection of books since the changes in 1989–90: Jens Bartelson, *A Genealogy of Sovereignty* (Cambridge: Cambridge University Press, 1995); Thomas Biersteker and Cynthia Weber, eds., *State Sovereignty as Social Construct* (Cambridge: Cambridge University Press, 1996); Joseph A. Camilleri and Jim Falk, eds., *End of Sovereignty? The Politics of a Shrinking and Fragmenting World* (Aldershot: Edward Elgar, 1992); Abram Chayes and Antonia Handler Chayes, *The New Sovereignty* (Cambridge: Harvard University Press, 1995); Jean L. Cohen, *Globalization and Sovereignty: Rethinking Legality, Legitimacy and Constitutionalism* (Cambridge: Cambridge University Press, 2012); Udo di Fabio, *Der Verfassungsstaat in der Weltgesellschaft* (Tübingen: Mohr Siebeck, 2001); Stephan Hobe, *Der offene Verfassungsstaat zwischen Souveränität und Interdependenz* (Berlin: Duncker & Humblot, 1998); John H. Jackson, *Sovereignty, the WTO, and Changing Fundamentals of International Law* (Cambridge: Cambridge University Press, 2006); Kalmo and Skinner, *Sovereignty in Fragments*; Jan Klabbers, Anne Peters, and Geir Ulfstein, *The Constitutionalization of International Law* (Oxford: Oxford University Press, 2009); Stephen D. Krasner, *Sovereignty: Organized Hypocrisy* (Princeton: Princeton University Press, 1999); Andrew Linklater, *The Transformation of Political Community: Ethical Foundations of the Post-Westphalian*

Era (Columbia: University of South Carolina Press, 1998); Daniel Loick, *Kritik der Souveränität* (Frankfurt: Campus, 2012); Neil MacCormick, *Questioning Sovereignty* (Oxford: Oxford University Press,1999); Andreas L. Paulus, *Die internationale Gemeinschaft im Völkerrecht: Eine Untersuchung zur Entwicklung des Völkerrechts im Zeitalter der Globalisierung* (Munich: Beck, 2001); Daniel Philpott, *Revolutions in Sovereignty: How Ideas Shaped Modern International Relations* (Princeton: Princeton University Press, 2001); Richard Rawlings, Peter Leyland, and Alison L. Young, eds., *Sovereignty and the Law* (Oxford: Oxford University Press, 2013); Utz Schliesky, *Souveränität und Legitimität von Herrschaftsgewalt* (Tübingen: Mohr Siebeck, 2004); Christian Seiler, *Der souveräne Verfassungsstaat zwischen demokratischer Rückbindung und überstaatlicher Einbindung* (Tübingen: Mohr Siebeck, 2005); Saskia Sassen, *Losing Control: Sovereignty in an Age of Globalization* (New York: Columbia University Press, 1996); Hendrik Spruyt, *The Sovereign State and Its Competitors: An Analysis of Systems Change* (Princeton: Princeton University Press, 1994); Neil Walker, ed., *Relocating Sovereignty* (Aldershot: Ashgate, 2006) and *Sovereignty in Transition* (Oxford: Hart, 2003).

3. See Martti Koskenniemi, "Conclusion: Vocabularies of Sovereignty—Powers of a Paradox," in Kalmo and Skinner, *Sovereignty in Fragments*, 222.

4. See, e.g., Kalmo and Skinner, *Sovereignty in Fragments*; Neil Walker, "Sovereignty Frames and Sovereignty Claims," in Rawlings, Leyland, and Young, *Sovereignty and the Law,* 18; Samantha Besson, "Sovereignty," in Rüdiger Wolfrum, ed., *Max Planck Encyclopedia of*

International Law (Oxford: Oxford University Press, 2011); Cohen, *Globalization and Sovereignty.*

5. Reinhart Koselleck, *Einleitung, Geschichtliche Grundbegriffe* (Stuttgart: Klett-Cotta, 1972), 1:xxii.

6. See Besson, "Sovereignty"; Anne Peters, "Membership in the Global Constitutional Community," in Klabbers, Peters and Ulfstein, *The Constitutionalization of International Law*, 153ff.

7. See Martti Koskenniemi, "The Fate of Public International law: Between Technique and Politics," *Modern Law Review* 70 (2007):1; Kalmo and Skinner, *Sovereignty in Fragments.*

8. Paul Laband, *Das Staatsrecht des Deutschen Reiches* (Tübingen: Mohr, 1876), 58f.

9. It is this situation that MacCormick, *Questioning Sovereignty*, 95, refers to as "post-sovereignty."

10. See Neil Walker, "Late Sovereignty in the European Union," in Walker, *Sovereignty in Transition*, 11ff.

11. See Karen J. Alter, *Establishing the Supremacy of European Law* (Oxford: Oxford University Press, 2001); Monica Claes, *The National Courts' Mandate in the European Constitution* (Oxford: Hart, 2006); Franz C. Mayer, *Kompetenzüberschreitung und Letztenscheidung* (Munich: Beck, 2000).

12. BVerfGE 123, 267 (2009)—Lisbon Treaty; BVerfGE 89, 155 (1993)— Maastricht Treaty.

13. "The concept of the union includes a close, long-term connection between still-sovereign states, which exercise public power on a treaty basis, but whose basic order is subject only to the direction of the

member states, and in which the peoples—that is, the citizens—of the member states remain the subjects of democratic legitimacy," BVerfGE 123, 267 (2009)—Lisbon Treaty.

14. Habermas's claim to the contrary does not find support in the text of the Lisbon Treaty; see Jürgen Habermas, *The Crisis of the European Union: A Response* (Cambridge: Polity, 2012), 12ff.; for a discussion of Habermas's view, Dieter Grimm, *Die Zukunft der Verfassung II* (Berlin: Suhrkamp, 2012), 128ff., 275ff.

15. BVerfGE 73, 339 (1986).

16. "Oublier la souveraineté pour penser le fédéralisme." Olivier Beaud, *Théorie de la Fédération* (Paris: Presses Universitaires de France, 2007), 58.

17. "Un ordre politique sans souveraineté," ibid., p.

18. Walker, "Late Sovereignty in the European Union," 14f.; see also Ulrich Haltern, *Was bedeutet Souveränität?* (Tübingen: Mohr Siebeck, 2007), 22; Martin Loughlin, "Why Sovereignty?" in Rawlings, Leyland, and Young, *Sovereignty and the Law,* 37.

19. See Stefan Oeter, *Integration und Subsidiarität im deutschen Bundesstaatsrecht* (Tübingen: Mohr Siebeck, 1998); Oeter, "Föderalismus," in Armin von Bogdandy, ed., *Europäisches Verfassungsrecht* (Berlin: Springer, 2003), 78ff.; Christoph Schönberger, "Die Europäische Union als Bund," *Archiv des öffentlichen Rechts* 129 (2004): 81; Anne Peters, *Elemente einer Theorie der Verfassung Europas* (Berlin: Duncker & Humblot, 2001), 144 ff.

20. Georg Waitz, "Das Wesen des Bundesstaats," *Allgemeine Monatsschrift für Wissenschaft und Literatur* (1853): 494ff.

21. See Dieter Grimm, "The State Monopoly of Force," in Wilhelm Heitmeyer and John Hagan, eds., *International Handbook of Violence Research* (Dordrecht: Springer, 2003), 1043.

22. See Neil Walker, "The Idea of Constitutional Pluralism," *Modern Law Review* 65 (2002): 317, and "Late Sovereignty in the European Union," where the citations are also found; Miguel Poires Maduro, "Contrapunctual Law: Constitutional Pluralism in Action," in Walker, *Sovereignty in Transition*, 502; also Catherine Richmond, "Preserving the Identity Crisis: Autonomy, System and Sovereignty in European Law," *Law and Philosophy* 16 (1997): 377; Mattias Kumm, "Who Is the Final Arbiter of Constitutionality in Europe?" *Common Market Law Review* 36 (1999): 351.

23. Maduro, "Contrapunctual Law," 526.

24. See Seyla Benhabib, *Another Cosmopolitanism* (Oxford: Oxford University Press, 2006); Lea Ypi, "Sovereignty, Cosmopolitanism and the Ethics of European Foreign Policy," *European Journal of Political Theory* 7 (2008): 349, and "Statist Cosmopolitanism," *Journal of Political Philosophy* 16 (2008): 48; Thomas Pogge, "Cosmopolitanism and Sovereignty," *Philosophy and Public Affairs* 33 (2005): 113.

25. See Lucius Caflisch, Torsten Stein, and Christian Tomuschat, eds., *Eingriff in die inneren Angelegenheiten fremder Staaten zum Zweck des Menschenrechtsschutzes* (Heidelberg: Müller, 2002); Gregory H. Fox and Brad R. Roth, eds., *Democratic Governance and International Law* (Cambridge: Cambridge University Press, 2000); J. L. Holzgrefe and Robert O. Keohane, eds., *Humanitarian Intervention: Ethical, Legal and Political Dilemmas* (Cambridge: Cambridge University Press, 2003); Mark Swatek-Evenstein, *Geschichte der humanitären Interven-*

tion (Baden-Baden: Nomos, 2008); Christopher Verlage, *Responsibility to Protect: Ein neuer Ansatz im Völkerrecht zur Verhinderung von Völkermord, Kriegsverbrechen und Verbrechen gegen die Menschlichkeit* (Tübingen: Mohr Siebeck, 2009).

26. Anne Peters, "Humanity as the A and O of Sovereignty," *European Journal of International Law* 20 (2009): 513.

27. See Cohen, *Globalization and Sovereignty*.

28. Peters, "Humanity as the A and O of Sovereignty," 541.

29. Cohen, *Globalization and Sovereignty*, 266.

30. But see Peters, "Dual Democracy," in Klabbers, Peters and Ulfstein, *The Constitutionalization of International Law*, 263ff.

31. As suggested in the titles of essays by J. H. H. Weiler, "Der Staat 'über alles,'" *Jahrbuch des Öffentlichen Rechts NF* 44 (1996): 91; and Miriam Aziz, "Sovereignty über alles," in Walker, *Sovereignty in Transition*, 280.

C. Sovereignty Today

Index

Court: French royal, 15; rights of, 18–19; *see also specific court*

Decision making: of people, 72; political, 40–41; power of final, 15; power of monarchy on, 26; sovereignty as final authority on, 14

Declaration of Colonial Rights and Grievances of the First Continental Congress, 35, 136*n*6

Declaration of Independence, U.S. (1776), 35, 136*n*6

De iure belli ac pacis (Grotius), 81

Democracy, 47, 72

Dispute Settlement Body (WTO), 87

Duguit, Léon, 6

East Germany, 67

ECJ, *see* European Court of Justice

Emperor: disputes with, 15; power of, 16, 25

England, 35; American Revolution and, 34; feudal system in, 24; as mixed government, 25; monarchy of, 25

English Parliament, 26; elements

of parliamentarism, 36; tariffs imposed by, 34

Estates, 27; rights of, 18–19, 25; rule of, 17

Estates-General, 24

Europe, 19–20, 27, 87

European Community law, primacy of, 89–91

European Convention on Human Rights, 87–88, 94

European Court of Human Rights, 88

European Court of Justice (ECJ), 89, 90–91, 97–98, 111–13, 127–28

European Monetary Union, 108

European Parliament, 89

European Union, xii, 6–7, 9, 71–72, 87–90, 95–96, 98, 107, 110–22; *see also* Common Market

External sovereignty: internal sovereignty and, 92–99; state and, 91–92; during twentieth century, 81–92; in Westphalian era, 77–81, 107–8

Faith, 19–20

Federal Convention, 36, 38, 57–58

North German Confederation;
    West Germany
Girard, Bernard de, 19
Glorious Revolution of 1688, 25
God, 13, 16–18, 22, 108
Government: legitimacy and shape
    of, 4; mixed, 21–22, 25, 32; self,
    49
Grotius, Hugo, 27, 81

Hague Convention Respecting the
    Laws and Customs of War on
    Land (1907), 82
Hague Peace Conference, 82
Hamilton, Alexander, 37, 52
Hänel, Albert, 65–66
Hayne, Robert, 52–53
Hegel, Georg Wilhelm Friedrich,
    49–50
Henry IV, 24
Hitler, Adolf, 67
Hobbes, Thomas, x, 28–30, 101
Holy Roman Empire, 25, 46; see also
    Reich
House of Commons, 25
House of Lords, 25
Huguenots, x, 27

Humanitarian intervention, 124
"Humanized sovereignty," 125–26
Human rights, 30–31, 85–88, 94,
    123–26

Indivisibility doctrine, 26, 38,
    69–70, 109–10, 114, 118, 152n9
Instrumentum Pacis Osnabrugensis,
    81
International cooperation: forms
    of, 87; legal order and, xi–xii,
    106–7
International Court of Justice, 86
International Covenant on Civil
    and Political Rights, 85
International Criminal Court, 91
International law, 7–8, 78–92,
    102–3, 124

Jackson, Andrew, 54
Jellinek, Georg, 7, 64–65
Jura summi imperii, see Sovereign
    rights
Jus cogens, 86
Justice, 22

Kelsen, Hans, 6, 66

UN Genocide Convention of 1948, 85

UN Security Council, 84–86

United Kingdom, 94

United Nations (UN), xii, 115–18, 121; articles of, 85; criminal tribunals of, 86; empowerment on use of force by, 84; formation of, 84; impact of, 87; members of, 84

United States of America (U.S.): customs law of, 56; federal laws of, 52–56; federal state and, 52–57; Force Bill of, 54; founding of, 34–36; South Carolina and, 52–56; sovereignty in, 50, 52–57; *see also* American Revolution

Universal Declaration of Human Rights (1948), xii, 85

U.S., *see* United States of America

U.S. Constitution, 34, 38, 52–56, 141*n*58

Vattel, Emer de, 33, 36

Waitz, Georg, 59–63, 114–15

Walker, Neil, 118, 128

Webster, Daniel, x, 53–55

Weimar Constitution, 48, 73, 75

West Germany, 67

Westphalian era, Westphalian order, 77–81, 87, 92, 107–8

Will: of God, 18; of sovereign, 21, 23

Wood, Gordon, 34

World Trade Organization (WTO), xii, 86–87, 121

World War I, 83

World War II, 67, 82–83

WTO, *see* World Trade Organization

Yugoslavia, 86

Zorn, Philipp, 63

Columbia Studies in Political Thought / Political History
Dick Howard, General Editor

PIERRE ROSANVALLON,
Democracy Past and Future, edited by Samuel Moyn (2006)

CLAUDE LEFORT,
Complications: Communism and the Dilemmas of Democracy, translated by Julian Bourg (2007)